The New
Suburbanization

The Eisenhower Center for the
Conservation of Human Resources
Studies in the New Economy

The New Suburbanization

Challenge to the Central City

Thomas M. Stanback, Jr.

WESTVIEW PRESS

BOULDER • SAN FRANCISCO • OXFORD

RECEIVED

FEB 3 1992

The Eisenhower Center for the Conservation of Human Resources
Studies in the New Economy

Published in 1991 in the United States of America by Westview Press, Inc., 5500 Central Avenue, Boulder, Colorado 80301, and in the United Kingdom by Westview Press, 36 Lonsdale Road, Summertown, Oxford OX2 7EW

Library of Congress Cataloging-in-Publication Data
Stanback, Thomas M., Jr.
   The new suburbanization : challenge to the central city / by
Thomas M. Stanback, Jr.
      p. cm. — (The Eisenhower Center for the Conservation of
Human Resources studies in the new economy)
   Includes index.
   ISBN 0-8133-8051-0
   1. Suburbs—United States. 2. Suburbs—Economic aspects—United
States. 3. Metropolitan areas—United States. 4. Inner cities—
United States. I. Title. II. Series.
HT352.U6S69 1991
307.74'0973—dc20   90-39827
                                                                  CIP

Printed and bound in the United States of America

The paper used in this publication meets the requirements
of the American National Standard for Permanence of Paper
for Printed Library Materials Z39.48-1984.

10   9   8   7   6   5   4   3   2   1

Contents

v

Tables

Foreword

I was very pleased when my long-term research associate and friend, Thomas Stanback, Jr., asked me to write a foreword for this book. During the more than quarter-century of our research association, I have learned a great deal about the urban scene from the books that Stanback has authored. *Suburbanization and the City* (1976), which he wrote in association with Richard Knight, served as a major eye-opener in enhancing my understanding of the symbiosis between the central business district (CBD) of our major metropolises and the bedroom communities where many of their workers slept.

Now, fifteen years later—a relatively short period of time in the history of even dynamic capitalistic economies—Stanback has taken a fresh look at fourteen metropolitan centers, including the four largest—New York, Chicago, Los Angeles, and Philadelphia—and has come up with some strikingly new and different findings and recommendations from those contained in his earlier study.

Stanback has not only been a pioneering student of urbanization but has also made important contributions to assessing the accelerating shift of the U.S. economy from goods to services. He has paid particular attention to the critical importance of business services in usurping the central role in the recent revitalization of so many of our larger central business districts in our older cities. The present volume builds on his dual areas of expertise, as shown in his earlier studies of suburbanization and those focused on the growing role of business services in the reshaping of the U.S. economy.

What are the important new findings contained in Stanback's neat and closely argued monograph that should be of interest and concern to all of us—employers, politicians, planners, researchers, workers, and job seekers?

The old symbiosis can no longer be taken for granted. It is not necessarily true that as the suburbs continue to gain population, the economic exchange between suburbanites commuting to the city for work and the continuing well-being of the central city will be assured. The "new" in *The New Suburbanization* refers to the fact that many, though not all, of the suburbs of our major cities have begun to enjoy the benefits of agglomeration—benefits formerly reserved only for cities—and accordingly the industrial composition, employment, and earnings profiles of the new suburbs may no longer be constrained by overemphasis on manufacturing, retailing, and other consumer services.

The new suburban agglomerations have been able to attract a wide range of business services—from finance, insurance, and real estate (FIRE) to research laboratories and often including hotel complexes, theaters, and convention sites—that make these suburban complexes direct competitors to CBDs. And these complexes have something very powerful going for them—the preference of more and more Americans to relocate away from the central city. But Stanback, having introduced this major revision to his earlier view of the symbiosis between city and suburb, is quick to add that not everything favors the new suburbs. Employers confront a tight labor market, particularly of young people reaching working age. The earnings profile remains unfavorable in the suburbs, across most industrial fields. Commuting within the suburban areas is increasingly gridlocked. Housing costs in many suburban areas are problematic for all except the more affluent members of the middle class.

But Stanback warns that these present and possibly worsening disabilities confronting the suburbs are no basis for satisfaction for those in most inner-cities, with their disproportionate numbers of low-income, less-educated populations; relatively low employment/population ratios; and a sharp divide between those who have jobs with an average salary of $25,000 and those who hold jobs with annual earnings of around $9,000.

Stanback is disturbed by the growing gap between the more successful and the less successful jobholders resident in the city. But his major concern is with poorly educated, minority youth, most of whom are not in the job market and who have little prospect of gaining entrance into any of the more demanding business service jobs that have come to constitute the expanding sector of the city's economy.

These urban youth cannot readily access the available unskilled jobs in the suburbs because of lack of private or public transportation. There is little prospect of the suburbs providing affordable housing for low-income persons. Hence it is essential for the city's future as well as for the future of these youth that efforts to improve their educational preparation be redoubled. The city needs more qualified workers, witness the continuing large flows of commuters who travel long distances every day to the CBDs. But the jobs in the CBDs increasingly require young people who have acquired a high school diploma, preferably a community college degree. High school dropouts and the functionally illiterate cannot handle these jobs.

No city can long prosper if it must support growing numbers of residents who are not capable of working. In fact such a city will see more and more of its employers desert. The symbiosis between the city and the new suburbs will be permanently upset unless the city—with the help of the federal and state governments—can assure that all of its potential workers are qualified to get and keep jobs. This is the important lesson that every reader should absorb from Stanback's insightful but upsetting tale.

Eli Ginzberg
The Eisenhower Center for the
Conservation of Human Resources,
Columbia University

Acknowledgments

Upon completion of a study, a staff member of the Conservation of Human Resources Project inevitably finds himself in debt to a number of colleagues for help and encouragement. In this case my thanks go first to Eli Ginzberg and Thierry Noyelle, who willingly read the manuscript at several stages and offered insightful criticism and advice. Thomas Bailey and Roger Waldinger also read the manuscript and made highly useful suggestions. Anna Dutka was helpful in many ways relating to source materials.

Greg Grove was a strong right arm in performing calculations and preparing tables. Shoshana Vasheetz and Brian Canivan typed the various drafts, and Charles Frederick was supportive in a variety of ways in expediting the flow of work. In the final stages Penny Peace edited the book effectively and with dispatch.

Finally, I would like to acknowledge with gratitude the financial assistance made possible by a grant from the Ford Foundation.

Thomas M. Stanback, Jr.

1

The Changing Metropolis

As we move into the final decade of the twentieth century, economists are focusing their attention on the central cities of our largest metropolitan economies where homelessness, unemployment, and poverty contrast sharply with the bustling prosperity of many central business districts. For the most part, however, their eyes remain diverted from the burgeoning suburbs, where the largest share of the U.S. populace is housed (46 percent, compared to 31 percent living within the municipal boundaries of central cities and 23 percent within nonmetropolitan areas)[1] and where, for decades, both employment and population have been growing at a more rapid pace.

Central Cities and Suburbs Within the
Metropolitan Economy: Symbiosis and Competition

In spite of their high visibility, central city economies do not stand alone. City and suburb, linked in a symbiotic yet competitive relationship, together constitute an economic system—the metropolitan economy. This symbiotic relationship is complex: The central city draws heavily upon the suburbs for its work force yet sends a substantial number of its resident workers daily to jobs outside its boundaries, and suburbs depend heavily upon the streams of income provided by the wages and salaries of commuters. Each subeconomy supplies the other with services and, to a lesser extent, with goods. Many suburban service and goods-producing organizations are branches of central city firms, often related in highly cost-effective intrafirm arrangements in which functions that require greater space and more routine labor, or that do not depend on the network of personal relationships possible within the city, are thrust outward to the suburbs.

Yet there is competition—competition for jobs and direct competition between central city and suburban firms themselves. For many firms in the city, suburban workers may be available as an alternative, and on

1

average a better-educated, labor supply. Moreover, the movement of firms to the suburbs or the establishment of branches or back offices reduces the demand for the city's labor. At the same time, the growth of the suburbs creates new outlying markets that justify the birth of new firms and nonprofit organizations, reduces the suburbs' reliance upon the city's firms and institutions as suppliers of goods and services, and broadens the locational options for firms.

It is in the very nature of the capitalistic system that firms continuously seek out new locational and operational strategies and new sources of labor. As the suburbs grow and develop, they open up new opportunities for firms and institutions to operate successfully in activities that were previously regarded as uneconomic. This suburban developmental process has been cumulative, driven not only by decades of relatively rapid suburban growth but by the major transformations that have taken place within the national economy. It is a major thesis of this study that the suburbs of large U.S. metropolises are today in the midst of a new phase of development—one that is more advanced than in the past—in which their economies are being significantly broadened, and that this development is altering the relationship between central cities and suburbs, bringing about new opportunities for both symbiosis and competition.

The Purpose and Plan of the Study

The principal objective of this study is to examine the changing structure of central cities and suburbs as reflected in the industrial composition and earnings of their work forces and to explore the implications of these developments on employment opportunities, especially for those minority groups within the central city that are most disadvantaged in gaining access to jobs that pay well and offer reasonable opportunities for advancement. The analysis treats both city and suburbs, contrasting employment characteristics and noting, where possible, differences in developmental patterns. Fourteen large metropolitan areas (see Table 1.5 for a list) are studied, with special emphasis given to the four largest, New York, Chicago, Philadelphia, and Los Angeles.

The following sections provide background for the analysis in subsequent chapters. The first highlights some of the principal factors that are transforming the U.S. economy and propelling rapid change and the restructuring of central cities and suburbs. The second briefly sketches the evolution of the suburbs from their early role as bedroom communities to their more complex development today. The third and fourth deal briefly with two major aspects of central city and suburban development:

employment and population change and the increasing importance of commuting.

Chapter 2 examines differences in the industrial composition of central cities and suburbs and analyzes patterns of change in the composition, structure, and functions of employment. Chapter 3 examines worker earnings in the various industry groups and discloses differences between central cities and suburbs as regards tendencies to upgrade activities through the use of better-paid and more skilled and experienced workers. Chapter 4 presents evidence of the development of new agglomerations of economic activity within the suburbs and assesses the significance of these new centers within the metropolitan economy. Chapter 5 analyzes a different data set for the four largest metropolitan areas in 1980 and 1985, comparing the labor force characteristics of central cities and suburbs. Chapter 6 examines the labor market problems of central cities and suburbs and considers several alternative approaches to bringing about increased employment and improved mobility of minorities.

Services, Technology, and the Changing Nature of Work

The growth and development of metropolitan economies are being driven by a larger transformation within the national economy and, indeed, within much of the world economy. This larger transformation has involved fundamental changes in what is produced, in how the processes of production are organized and carried out, and in the nature of work and the demand for labor.

In terms of what is being produced, there has been a major shift toward educational, health, and public services as well as the introduction of a variety of new private-sector consumer services.

In terms of how we produce, there have been fundamental changes in the way productive activity of all types is carried out—changes involving greater emphasis on planning, product design, distribution, finance, merchandising, advertising, government, and public and customer relations. These new arrangements have brought about a spectacular rise in the importance of a variety of intermediate services, including transportation, communication, wholesaling, finance, and various professional services such as accounting, legal counseling, management consulting, and advertising. The share of gross national product originating from these intermediate services has risen from 29 percent in 1947 to over 40 percent today.[2]

Although a number of factors have contributed to these transformations, including the opening up of broad national and world markets, improvements in transportation, increases in purchasing power, and the role of women in both the marketplace and the labor force, it is important to recognize that a major factor, both as cause and catalyst, has been the dramatic development of the new electronic technology.

The new service economy, coupled with the rapid adaptation of computer-telecommunications technology, has wrought fundamental changes in the nature of work. Blue-collar factory employment has declined at the same time that design, planning, control, and managerial functions have risen in importance within manufacturing firms, and the increasing importance of intermediate services has created a host of new employment opportunities for white-collar workers. To this has been added the increasing need for managerial, professional, sales, clerical, and service personnel in the social and consumer services.

Although computerization has simplified many tasks, there is surprisingly little evidence of de-skilling. To the contrary, what is taking place within many firms and organizations is a trend toward the elimination of routine work and a redefinition of jobs. Workers are being moved from the performance of repetitive "dog work" to assignments involving broader responsibilities and a greater knowledge of the employing organization, its policies, and its customers. With greater capability to build data bases relating to customers and operations and to communicate such information instantly throughout the organization there has been a need for reorganization, resulting in a "de-layering" in which skills and responsibilities are being pushed further down the corporate hierarchy.[3] At the same time, those smaller firms supplying the needs of larger corporations have been called upon to render a variety of services that require a high degree of flexibility and attention to customer needs, necessitating, once again, a greater measure of individual worker knowledge and responsibility.

This new demand for labor has brought about a new emphasis on the need for a better-educated and better-trained worker. At least some college training is increasingly a requirement for positions that offer some promise of advancement. When college training is not a prerequisite, firms increasingly demand a high school diploma as evidence of an ability to function effectively. Recent research reveals that across a broad spectrum of industries firms are moving toward the institution of strong training programs for all employees, including part-time workers, and are screening applicants with greater rigor in an effort to employ only those who possess the levels of literacy, numeracy, and social skills that will enable them to be "trainable" and, ultimately, productive employees.[4]

A fundamental aspect of the new service economy has been a trend toward the spatial de-coupling of factory production and other functions in the economic process. With improved highway, rail, air, and sea transport, manufacturing plants have tended to move away from heavily settled, high-cost areas to more rural settings or to overseas locations. At the same time, intermediate services, headquarters, and distribution activities have located within the metropolitan area in closer proximity to their major markets, to a rich and varied labor force—and to each other.

But there have been other forces of centralization and decentralization at work as well. Advances in computer-telecommunications technology have increasingly made it possible to centralize the production of certain services (e.g., back-office activity of insurance companies and software design) away from those places at which the service is made available in the marketplace. At the same time, the new technology makes possible a customization of the firm's output to meet the special needs of the buyer, increasing the importance of locating the activities involved in the sale and delivery of services closer to the major markets to be served. All this broadens the range of locational choice.

Changes in the Nature of Suburban Growth and Development

The earlier development of the suburbs arose principally out of two sets of forces. The first was the movement of city residents to the suburbs in search of lower costs of living and more spacious living arrangements. The second was the movement of manufacturing from city to suburbs in response to the dual attraction of new and cheaper transportation arrangements, as the highway system expanded and trucking offered a lower-cost transportation option to railways, coupled with the search for cheaper building sites to house the new one-story industrial structures that were proving to be more efficient than the old multistoried plants. Both developments brought dramatic increases in population and with them a demand for new retail stores, new public services, and a host of other for-profit and not-for-profit services.

As such growth continued, expanding market size within the suburbs encouraged import substitution, which gave further impetus to economic development. City-based retailers established suburban outlets; hospitals and colleges were built; banks, legal offices, and other business service firms were opened up. Increasingly, suburban residents and businesses no longer found it necessary to import these services from the central city.

The most recent phase of economic development in the suburbs has involved the building of the export sector. The old export sector—manufacturing in some suburbs and everywhere the daily "export" of commuters' services to the central city—remains important. But economic growth today arises in large measure out of the establishment of new export activities. Examples of a strengthening of the suburban export base through growth of service activities abound especially in wholesaling and business-related services. Further evidence is readily observed if one ventures forth into the suburbs: the fine new hotels offering conference facilities as well as accommodations to salespeople, visiting executives, and tourists alike; the numerous office parks and freestanding facilities that house divisional offices and sales centers of large corporations and back-office adjuncts to banks and insurance companies; laboratories and research and development centers; and, not infrequently, corporate head-quarters. In many instances, high-tech industrial and office complexes have flourished in areas well removed from the city but, nevertheless, also well within the metropolitan orbit (e.g., the Route 128, Princeton, and Philadelphia suburban complexes).

But not all suburban areas have developed to the same extent or in the same way. As will be shown in Chapter 4, some suburban counties have become centers of retail and commercial activities, some of research and development or high-tech production, and some are manufacturing centers. Many, however, remain largely residential areas.

Moreover, the relationship between central city and suburbs will be shown to vary. In some instances, the city develops by becoming the center for new and more advanced services while the suburbs develop by gaining those services erstwhile performed in the city but now more appropriately located in the suburbs. Here symbiosis is dominant and competition minimal. In other instances, the city continues to dominate as the focal point of export-oriented activities while the suburbs perform largely residentiary related functions and are providers of skilled workers. Again, competition and conflict are minimal and symbiosis of a sort is dominant. But there are still other metropolitan areas in which the suburbs, or more accurately centers within the suburbs, are building rapidly at the expense of the central city economy. It is largely here that the problems of the city are exacerbated, particularly as they relate to providing employment for the hard to employ.

Population and Employment Growth

In the late 1970s, considerable attention was given to what appeared to be a new trend toward dispersion of people and economic activity within the U.S. economy: Population in nonmetropolitan counties taken as a whole had grown more rapidly during the decade than in metropolitan counties (Table 1.1). What went largely unnoticed, however, was that within metropolitan areas suburban counties had grown at a considerably more rapid rate than had nonmetropolitan counties, although central cities—in part as a result of difficult transformations in many of the

Table 1.1   Annual Growth Rates of Metropolitan and Nonmetropolitan Population, 1970–1980, 1980–1987

	1970–1980	1980–1987
Metropolitan	1.00	1.12
Central city	0.08	0.74
Suburbs	1.74	1.37
Nonmetropolitan counties	1.34	0.58
≥ 15% commute to metro	1.80	1.21
10–14% commute to metro	1.48	0.78
5–9% commute to metro	1.33	0.63
< 5% commute to metro	1.24	0.42
Metropolitan, by population size		
> 5 million	0.33	0.97
1–5 million	1.09	1.23
250,000–1 million	1.38	1.17
< 250,000	1.60	1.03

Source: U.S. Bureau of the Census, Current Population Reports, series P-23, no. 159, Population Profile of Employment and Unemployment, 1989 (Washington, DC: GPO, 1989).

larger places—had grown very little or declined (Table 1.1). Moreover, subsequent analysis has revealed that it was in those nonmetropolitan counties in which there was significant commuting into the metropolitan areas that growth was most rapid (Table 1.1). Since the beginning of the 1980s, the trend toward the increasing importance of metropolitan areas has been reaffirmed: Growth in the nonmetropolitan U.S. population has slowed sharply while growth in metropolitan areas has accelerated, principally because of growth in the suburbs.

Within metropolitan areas, employment in both central city and suburbs has tended to grow more rapidly than population, with employment in suburbs typically outpacing that of central cities. (See Table 1.2 for evidence based on the experience of the fourteen central cities and suburbs examined in this study.) Low rates of employment growth in cities have in many instances been due to substantial declines in some industries (principally manufacturing) that at least partially offset gains in others. On the other hand, job increases in the suburbs have typically occurred at much faster rates, with negligible or no job decreases.

The tendency for suburbs to grow more rapidly than cities is not a recent development. Wide differentials in growth rates occurred as well during the 1940s, 1950s, and 1960s. Table 1.3, from an earlier study of a selected group of major U.S. cities,[5] shows average annual growth rates for population and employment in two major industrial sectors, manufacturing and retailing, over the 1940–1970 period.

Table 1.2   Annual Rates of Employment and Population Change and Job Decrease/
Job Increase Ratios (JD/JI), 1969–1987

	Employment[a]				Population	
	City		Suburbs		Rate of Change	
	JD/JI[a]	Rate of Change	JD/JI[a]	Rate of Change	City	Suburbs
New York	1.23	−0.20	0.02	2.55	−0.40	0.12
Chicago	0.65	0.40	0.02	4.00	−0.19	1.99
Philadelphia	3.98	−1.20	0.12	2.46	−0.95	0.75
Los Angeles	—[b]	2.20	0.05	5.70	1.10	2.69
Atlanta	0.03	2.10	0.00	5.87	0.23	3.68
Boston	0.63	0.50	0.02	2.50	−0.53	0.24
Cincinnati	0.28	1.10	0.00	3.60	−0.27	1.16
Columbus	0.09	2.60	0.04	1.70	0.68	1.36
Dallas	0.00	3.70	0.00	6.30	2.06	5.68
Detroit	4.82	−1.00	0.05	3.20	−1.22	1.00
Minneapolis	0.01	2.50	0.07	2.90	0.16	1.75
Pittsburgh	0.85	0.20	0.54	0.60	−0.91	0.01
St. Louis	9.44	−1.70	0.00	2.90	−2.31	0.87
Washington	0.35	0.60	0.02	4.30	−1.12	1.73
U.S.	0.04	2.18				

[a] Employment change was netted out for each major industry group. JI is the sum of increases; JD is the sum of decreases. JD/JI is a ratio.
[b] Less than .001.

Source: Data supplied by the Bureau of Economic Analysis.

Accordingly, the suburban economies of the late 1980s must be seen in light of more than four decades of sustained growth. Older, simplistic views of the suburbs as largely residential extensions of the city must give way to a view of these areas as economies in the process of becoming increasingly complex and mature. Yet we shall observe in the subsequent analysis that suburbs have faced significant constraints in terms of the extent to which they have been able to upgrade the earnings levels of their work forces as compared to those of the cities.

Importance of Commuting

Commuting has increased rapidly in the U.S. economy in recent decades, rising from about 39 million to roughly 68 million between the census years 1960 and 1980.[6]

In a recent study of commuting in the United States, Alan Pisarski noted the following trends for the 1960–1980 period:[7]

Table 1.3   Average Annual Growth Rates of Central City and Suburb Population and
of Manufacturing and Retailing Employment, 1940–1970

	1940–1950		1950–1960		1960–1970	
	City	Suburb	City	Suburb	City	Suburb
Population	0.80	4.19	−0.21	6.78	−0.54	3.35
Employment						
Manufacturing	10.39	12.16	−1.13	5.02	−0.04	4.21
Retailing	4.74	8.40	−0.52	7.69	−1.33	7.48

Note: Average growth rates of eight large metropolitan areas are modified. Highest and
lowest rates have been dropped and averages computed.

Source: Thomas M. Stanback, Jr., and Richard V. Knight, *Suburbanization and the City*
(Montclair, NJ: Allanheld, Osmun & Co., 1976).

1. The most important increases in commuting were in intrasuburban
   movements with the number of commuters rising from 11 million
   to over 25 million, resulting in an increase in share of total flows
   from 28 to 38 percent. Commuting to destinations outside the
   metropolitan areas (predominantly by suburban residents) also
   increased (from about 2 to 7 percent of total flows).
2. "Traditional" suburb-to-central-city movements almost doubled,
   gaining about 6 million workers and increasing the share from 16
   to 19 percent of total flows.
3. "Reverse" commuting (city to suburb) rose but remained at about
   5 to 6 percent of total flows.
4. Commuter movements within the central city declined sharply in
   share, from about 46 to 30 percent.

Analysis of the Residence Adjustment Data

The increasing importance of commuting in cities and suburbs is
readily observed in Table 1.4, based on the residence adjustment estimates
of the Bureau of Economic Analysis (BEA). These estimates, which are
available for as late as 1987, are prepared and published annually on
a county basis and may be consolidated to conform with the city and
suburb definitions used in this study. They are estimates of *net* commuter
earnings (the earnings of out-commuters minus the earnings of in-
commuters). To estimate earnings of workers at place of residence, the
BEA uses net commuter earnings to adjust county estimates of total
worker earnings at place of work. Where in-commuter earnings exceed
out-commuter earnings, the residence adjustment is negative (it is de-
ducted from total earnings at place of work in estimating total resident
earnings). Conversely, where out-commuter earnings exceed in-commuter

Table 1.4 Residence Adjustment as a Percentage of Total Earnings at Place of Work, 1969, 1987

	Central City			Suburbs		
	1969	1987	Change	1969	1987	Change
New York	−23.2	−28.5	−	47.1	30.7	−
Chicago	−9.7	−15.0	−	48.6	43.9	−
Philadelphia	−29.0	−33.2	−	31.6	22.8	−
Los Angeles	−7.4	−11.4	−	32.9	15.4	−
Atlanta	−39.3	−48.3	−	51.9	34.2	−
Boston	−50.2	−52.6	−	16.6	6.7	−
Cincinnati	−19.4	−25.9	−	104.0	70.2	−
Columbus	−6.9	−12.8	−	18.8	39.9	+
Dallas	−10.5	−23.9	−	69.4	118.3	+
Detroit	−16.2	−19.2	−	32.9	20.9	−
Minneapolis	−11.5	−21.7	−	11.5	24.4	+
Pittsburgh	−8.6	−12.3	−	24.9	27.6	+
St. Louis	−52.8	−52.8	=	38.2	15.4	−
Washington	−54.0	−61.5	−	46.5	19.6	−

Note: Residence adjustment is computed by subtracting in-commuter from out-commuter earnings. Negative sign (−) indicates net in-commuter earnings; positive sign (+) indicates net out-commuter earnings.

Source: Data supplied by the Bureau of Economic Analysis.

earnings the residence adjustment is positive (it is added to total earnings at place of work in estimating total resident earnings).

In Table 1.4, the residence adjustments are shown as percentages of total worker earnings (place of work) for the years 1969 and 1987 with minus or plus signs shown to indicate net in-commuter or net out-commuter earnings, respectively. An initial finding is that the residence adjustment is negative for every central city in both years; positive for every suburb.

The rather wide range of percentages of residence adjustment to total earnings of workers employed in the cities—from 11 to 60 percent in 1987—should not be regarded as necessarily indicative of differences among cities in the importance of commuting. At least in part they are accounted for by variations in the extent to which central city counties overbound the cities themselves. For example, Cook County, the central city county, overbounds the city of Chicago to a considerable extent. Accordingly, the flow of commuting into the county fails to reveal the full extent of commuting into the city because it does not include the large flow of out-of-city commuters who live within the county. Ratios of city-to-county population (Table 1.5) indicate a fairly high correspondence between overbounding (i.e., low ratios of city to central county

Table 1.5   Population of Central Cities and Central City Counties, 1980

	Central City	Central City County	City-to-County Population Ratio
New York	7,072	7,072	1.00
Chicago	3,005	5,256	0.57
Philadelphia	1,688	1,688	1.00
Los Angeles	2,967	7,504	0.40
Atlanta	425	592	0.72
Boston	563	651	0.86
Cincinnati	385	873	0.44
Columbus	565	871	0.65
Dallas	904	1,566	0.58
Detroit	1,203	2,329	0.52
Minneapolis	371	944	0.39
Pittsburgh	424	1,448	0.29
St. Louis	453	453	1.00
Washington	638	638	1.00

Source: U.S. Bureau of the Census, Census of Population, 1980 (Washington, DC: GPO, 1980). Central city data from U.S. Bureau of the Census, Statistical Abstract of the United States, 1984 (Washington, DC: GPO, 1984). Central city county data supplied by the Bureau of Economic Analysis.

residents) and low residence adjustment ratios (Table 1.4). It seems clear that if net inflows of commuters to cities were properly measured they would be substantial in virtually all places.

A second finding is that resident adjustment ratios became increasingly negative in all cities from 1969 to 1987, indicating a general trend toward an increasing role played by in-commuters in central city economies.

Paradoxically, the residence adjustment measure also declined in most suburbs (ten of the fourteen), indicating a declining importance of out-commuter earnings as a source of income within these economies. The paradox is explained by the much more rapid growth of the suburbs and the fact that they increasingly are receiving in-commuters from outlying areas. In spite of the larger number of commuters moving into the city daily, this larger net outflow from the suburbs accounts for a smaller percentage of the total number of persons working in the suburbs.

Commuting Measures

Measures based on estimates of the number of commuters are presented in Table 1.6. Only in-commuter measures are shown except for cities in 1980 because out-commuter measures were subject to error, as significant numbers of residents failed to indicate place of work when the "Journey to Work" questions in the Census of Population were asked. BEA-corrected estimates of city out-commuting in 1980 are available,

Table 1.6 Selected Measures of Commuting, 1960, 1980

| | City | | | Suburbs | |
| | In-Commuters as Percentage of Work Force | | Ratio of Out-Commuters to In-Commuters | In-Commuters as Percentage of Work Force | |
	1960	1980	1980	1960	1980
New York	17.90	20.40	0.28	15.70	23.50
Chicago	6.60	13.30	0.40	31.00	31.00
		(31.20)[a]	(0.50)[a]		
Philadelphia	23.50	32.10	0.37	22.70	29.60
Los Angeles	3.70	9.50	0.41	9.80	14.30
		(38.20)[a]	(0.64)[a]		
Atlanta	28.80	58.00	0.17	17.60	36.80
Boston	54.40	55.60	0.26	18.20	25.90
Cincinnati	19.80	27.40	0.19	19.40	19.10
Columbus	7.00	12.40	0.28	10.10	20.50
Dallas	6.90	19.80	0.21	4.50	19.30
Detroit	14.90	23.10	0.68	21.30	28.20
Minneapolis	12.20	26.80	0.40	21.40	36.00
Pittsburgh	8.10	15.40	0.33	13.80	18.60
St. Louis	40.90	63.30	0.19	18.10	23.40
Washington	45.60	64.60	0.15	25.80	41.10

[a] Computed from "Journey to Work" data from the 1980 Census of Population using city rather than county definitions of central cities.

Note: Out-commuter data for 1960 are not shown because they are subject to error due to failure of some resident workers to indicate place of work; however, these data were provided with estimated corrections for cities in 1980 and were used for city ratios of out-commuters to in-commuters.

Source: Data supplied by the Bureau of Economic Analysis.

however, and were used to compute ratios of out-commuters and in-commuters for that year.

The commuting measures support the finding that central city economies have become increasingly dependent on commuters in recruiting their work forces: The percentage of the work force accounted for by in-commuters increased significantly from 1960 to 1980 in every one of the fourteen cities. We observe also that out-commuting from the city is important everywhere but is well below the level of in-commuting.

Central city measures based on correct municipal boundaries prepared from "Journey to Work" data are shown in Table 1.6 for Chicago and Los Angeles, the two major cities for which county boundaries significantly overbound the municipality. New York and Philadelphia are, as noted earlier, defined properly by county boundaries. These estimates show that the relative importance of both in-commuting and out-commuting in Chicago and Los Angeles is much greater than the measures based on county definition would indicate. We also note that Los Angeles stands apart in that commuter flows out of the city are much larger relative to commuter flows into the city (64 percent) than is the case of any of the other central cities.

An additional finding sheds light on the significance of the declining levels of *net* out-commuter earnings in most of the suburbs that were observed in the residence adjustment data: The percentage of the work force accounted for by in-commuters increased in twelve of the fourteen suburbs. Increases in the number of in-commuters raises the level of in-commuter earnings and accordingly acts to decrease *net* out-commuter earnings. The increase of in-commuters also helps to explain why suburban employment gains have outpaced population growth.

The Data

The analysis in Chapters 2 and 3 is based largely on employment and earnings data for major industry groups published by the BEA, supplemented in several instances by more detailed *County Business Patterns* (CBP) employment data published by the Bureau of the Census.

The residence adjustment and commuter data presented in the present chapter and in Chapter 3 were estimated by the BEA and are benchmarked on *Census of Population* "Journey to Work" data.

With minor exceptions, all data utilized in this and the next three chapters are county data. The central cities of New York, Philadelphia, St. Louis, and Washington, D.C., are coterminous with a county or counties (the five boroughs of New York City are counties), so for these places use of county data poses no difficulty. In the case of the remaining cities—including two major cities, Chicago and Los Angeles—this procedure is open to criticism because the central city county substantially overbounds the municipal limits of the central city. The city of Chicago accounts for but 57 percent of the population of Cook County, and the city of Los Angeles for only 40 percent of Los Angeles County population. Table 1.5 compares municipal population with central city county population.

Yet all of these central cities do, indeed, dominate their counties. Given that employment data at place of work are available only on a county basis, there is no alternative but to use them, recognizing that central city county employment and population may provide only a rough approximation of the central city itself.

With two exceptions, New York and Los Angeles, the suburbs of the metropolitan areas are simply the combined remaining counties of the Primary Metropolitan Statistical Area (PMSA). In the case of the New York suburbs, the counties of Nassau, Suffolk, and Bergen (which were previously included in the metropolitan-area definition) were added to the PMSA. In the case of Los Angeles, there are no remaining counties as Los Angeles County alone comprises the PMSA. Here Orange County, which sends a substantial number of commuters into Los Angeles, was used as a surrogate suburban area.

In Chapter 5, data from the *Census of Population Survey* are examined for the four largest metropolitan areas. Here the outer bounds of the metropolitan areas are defined as above, but cities are correctly delimited by their municipal boundaries and suburban areas make up the remaining areas.

The New Suburbanization and the Challenge
to the Central City

In an earlier study,[8] the author and a colleague, Richard Knight, examined the development of larger central cities and their suburbs during the period of 1960–1970, resulting in a number of findings, including the following:

1. The slow job improvement or outright decline of central city employment, largely in manufacturing, at the same time that suburban economies were developing rapidly.

2. The development of new institutional arrangements, particularly industrial and office parks, that were strengthening suburban economies and moving them away from an earlier role as merely bedroom communities.

3. The continued importance of commuting to the central city as a source of primary income for the suburbs and the continued

importance of suburban residentiary activities to provide for the combined domestic needs of those who worked in the city and those employed locally.

4. The higher levels of wages paid in many activities in the central city, although not necessarily in manufacturing.

5. The higher rates of labor force participation and more abundant job opportunities for young workers in the suburbs, although gains for black workers were less clearly indicated. For blacks in both cities and suburbs, opportunities for employment in the burgeoning suburbs were found to be seriously diminished by the spatial diffusion of the suburban economy and associated difficulties of transportation.

At one point in the analysis it was stated:

A central theme clearly emerges . . . : patterns of change within metropolitan economies are similar everywhere. They involve a restructuring of the city which favors business services and involves an upgrading of activities— an expansion of business services and a decline of manufacturing and local-sector employment. At the same time, they involve a growth and restructuring of the suburbs which favor high value-added manufacturing and the buildup of a disproportionally large consumer sector to service a populace which is on balance more affluent than that of the city.

. . . Moreover, in cities, the process is one in which restructuring comes about through job creation and job destruction against a background in which the positive forces (evident in the expanding business services) are often obscured by the more dramatic loss of blue-collar jobs in manufacturing. . . .

This affects the suburbs, since the relationship is symbiotic. Its local sector depends heavily upon the welfare of its "hidden export" sector (i.e., commuter wages and salaries). Its export sector in manufacturing and even back office activities requires a strong city service base, nearby urban amenities, a thriving market within the general metropolitan region, and the availability of first-rate metropolitan transportation facilities.[9]

In large measure, these observations continue to hold, but there are significant differences. The two recent decades have brought a number of important changes:

1. The remarkable transformation of the U.S. economy, involving major shifts in the industrial composition of employment from goods to services.

2. The transformation of our largest central cities, involving a re-building of the central business district and an upgrading of key service activities.
3. Almost twenty years of continuous growth along with major restructuring of the export base, which has created far more diversified and vibrant suburban economies than existed in 1970. Although it is true that industrial parks and office parks were very much in evidence in the early 1970s, they were essentially an incipient development compared to what is observed today. Major quantitative change has brought major qualitative change. The new suburbanization is bringing about the creation of large centers of economic activity and the development of agglomeration economies (described in Chapter 4) that place the suburbs in sharper competition with central cities than was formerly the case.
4. The decline in the demand for poorly educated workers and the significant rise in the demand for better-educated workers. Jobs traditionally available to disadvantaged minority workers have declined and rates of their unemployment have worsened.

Thus, there has developed a new suburbanization at the same time that central cities have become in many ways transformed and revitalized. There is both a new symbiosis and a new competition between central cities and their suburbs. These major changes have brought in their wake new problems and new challenges.

Notes

1. Estimates supplied by the Bureau of Economic Analysis.
2. Thierry Noyelle, "Economic Transformation," *Annals* 488(November 1986):11.
3. For a fuller discussion of these trends, see Thierry J. Noyelle, *Beyond Industrial Dualism: Market and Job Segmentation in the New Economy* (Boulder, CO: Westview Press, 1986).
4. Lauren Benton, Thomas Bailey, Thierry Noyelle, and Thomas Stanback, Jr., *Training and Competitiveness in U.S. Manufacturing and Services: Training Needs and Practices by Lead Firms in Textiles, Banking, Retailing, and Business Services* (Boulder, CO: Westview Press, forthcoming).
5. Thomas M. Stanback, Jr., and Richard V. Knight, *Suburbanization and the City* (Montclair, NJ: Allanheld, Osmun & Co., 1976), pp. 56–57.
6. Alan E. Pisarski, *Commuting in America* (Washington, DC: Eno Foundation for Transportation, 1987), p. 34.
7. Pisarski, *Commuting in America.*
8. Stanback and Knight, *Suburbanization and the City.*
9. Stanback and Knight, *Suburbanization and the City.*

2

The Industrial Composition
of Employment

To a large extent, the kinds of jobs available to workers in cities and suburbs depend on the industrial mix of these economies—what goods and services they produce. This chapter examines industrial mix as measured in terms of employment composition—what percentage of all workers are employed in each major industrial group. Patterns of specialization—i.e., the relative concentration of employment in given industries—are noted and compared between cities and suburbs, and the changes in specialization from the beginning of the 1970s until the late 1980s are discussed.

In Chapter 3, a second dimension of economic specialization will be examined: the extent to which value added, as represented by average worker earnings, varies among industries and between city and suburb.

A First Look at City-Suburban
Industrial Composition

A useful measure of industrial specialization is the location quotient (LQ)—the ratio of the share of employment accounted for by an industry in a given location to the corresponding share of employment of that industry in the U.S. economy as a whole. For example, New York City, with 14.68 percent of its total employment in finance, insurance, and real estate (FIRE) compared to 7.95 percent within the U.S. economy, has an LQ of 1.85 and is regarded as heavily specialized. Detroit, with a corresponding LQ of .85, is not. LQ measures for the fourteen central cities studied here are presented in Table 2.1.

Among the fourteen central cities, the LQs indicate considerable variation in the structure of employment. Yet there are three industrial groups in which most central cities are overrepresented when compared to the U.S. economy—wholesaling, FIRE, and other services. In most cases,

Table 2.1 Percentage Distribution of U.S. Employment by Industry and Location Quotients, 1987

	Percentage	Location Quotient[a]								
	U.S.	New York	Chicago	Philadelphia	Los Angeles	Atlanta	Boston	Cincinnati	Columbus	Dallas
City										
Construction	5.50	0.62	0.70	0.45	0.70	0.74	0.47	0.86	0.85	0.98
Manufacturing	15.51	0.62	1.06	0.72	1.22	0.55	0.40	1.31	0.71	0.90
TCU	4.85	1.21	1.24	1.11	0.94	1.93	1.18	1.00	0.89	1.35
Wholesale	4.97	1.26	1.51	1.07	1.29	1.95	0.86	1.35	1.06	1.65
Retail	16.83	0.65	0.92	0.81	0.87	0.82	0.63	0.97	1.15	0.94
FIRE	7.95	1.85	1.22	1.20	1.11	1.30	1.84	1.00	1.42	1.54
Other services	26.74	1.29	1.08	1.26	1.15	1.11	1.47	1.06	1.03	0.98
Federal, civilian government	2.49	0.78	0.79	2.64	0.60	1.31	1.33	0.67	0.76	0.76
State, local government	11.14	1.08	0.82	0.87	0.77	0.85	1.10	0.74	1.19	0.59
Other	4.01[c]									
	100.00									
Suburbs										
Construction	5.50	1.07	1.14	1.08	1.07	1.47	1.01	1.25	1.06	1.39
Manufacturing	15.51	0.90	0.94	1.10	1.19	0.87	1.21	0.85	1.53	1.05
TCU	4.85	0.90	1.19	0.90	0.58	1.25	0.72	1.14	0.75	0.67
Wholesale	4.97	1.60	1.46	1.19	1.02	1.72	1.21	0.70	0.43	0.64
Retail	16.83	0.99	1.07	1.05	1.01	1.14	1.01	1.38	1.06	1.18
FIRE	7.95	1.00	0.96	1.01	1.44	1.03	0.84	0.68	0.80	1.02
Other services	26.74	1.14	1.16	1.08	1.06	0.85	1.17	0.99	0.84	0.89
Federal, civilian government	2.49	0.50	0.23	0.55	0.47	0.82	0.57	1.03	1.04	0.29
State, local government	11.14	0.88	0.65	0.70	0.62	0.77	0.67	0.96	1.17	1.26
Other	4.01[c]									
	100.00									

	Percentage	Location Quotient[a]						Tallies	
	U.S.	Detroit	Minneapolis	Pittsburgh	St. Louis	Washington	Average[b]	C>S	LQ>1.0
City									
Construction	5.50	0.54	0.78	0.98	0.58	0.40	0.69	0	0
Manufacturing	15.51	1.46	0.97	0.72	1.04	0.15	0.85	4	5
TCU	4.85	1.19	1.17	0.96	1.62	0.73	1.16	11	9
Wholesale	4.97	1.07	1.54	1.08	1.31	0.24	1.25	10	12
Retail	16.83	0.95	0.97	1.09	0.71	0.47	0.86	1	2
FIRE	7.95	0.85	1.29	1.05	1.10	0.80	1.24	11	11
Other services	26.74	1.00	1.09	1.31	1.09	1.38	1.15	12	12
Federal, civilian government	2.49	0.70	0.70	0.85	2.80	11.21	1.17	12	5
State, local government	11.14	0.99	0.77	0.69	0.70	0.65	0.84	10	3
Other	4.01[c]								
	100.00								
								S>C	LQ>1.0
Suburbs									
Construction	5.50	0.82	1.02	1.13	1.10	1.45	1.15	14	13
Manufacturing	15.51	1.39	1.30	1.09	1.07	0.26	1.08	10	9
TCU	4.85	0.61	0.91	1.25	1.05	0.99	0.93	3	5
Wholesale	4.97	0.99	0.83	0.98	1.01	0.79	1.03	4	7
Retail	16.83	1.15	1.10	1.20	1.13	1.02	1.09	13	13
FIRE	7.95	0.93	0.91	0.59	0.95	1.03	0.93	3	5
Other services	26.74	1.08	0.96	0.98	1.07	1.19	1.04	2	8
Federal, civilian government	2.49	0.54	0.49	0.36	0.59	3.59	0.60	2	3
State, local government	11.14	0.69	1.02	0.94	0.68	1.00	0.85	4	3
Other	4.01[c]								
	100.00								

[a] Location quotient is the ratio of the share of employment in a given industry group to the corresponding share in U.S. employment.

[b] Modified average: highest and lowest values dropped.

[c] Includes primary industries and military.

Note: Other services include business-related services (SICs 73, 81, 89); repair services (SICs 75, 76); social services (SICs 80, 82, 84, 86); consumer services (SICs 70, 72, 78, 79).

Source: Data supplied by the Bureau of Economic Analysis.

these cities are heavily overrepresented (LQs of 1.35 or more) in one or more of these industry groups—demonstrating their role as specialized producers of services destined for users throughout the region or beyond.

The low LQs for retailing in virtually all central cities attest to another shared characteristic. Because many in the city's work force are commuters who live elsewhere, the role of the central city's economy as a provider of residentiary services is more limited than in the suburbs and, consequently, a smaller share of the work force is engaged in retail activities.

The findings for the suburbs are quite different. In thirteen of the fourteen suburbs, the LQs indicate above average concentration in two industry groups, construction and retailing. In construction, relatively high employment shares reflect, at least in part, the effect of higher population and employment growth rates—a manifestation of the time-honored "acceleration principle" of economics: The *level* of investment activity (in this case, construction) is a function of the *rate* of growth.[1] In the case of retailing, the converse of what was found for city economies is observed: Suburban economies must provide for the needs not only of the families of residents who live and work in the outlying areas of the metropolis but also of the substantial number who work in the city. In addition, suburbs tend to have larger manufacturing sectors than cities. LQs for nine of the fourteen suburbs are well above 100; in ten, they are higher than for the corresponding central cities.

The importance of wholesaling varies. In the New York, Chicago, Philadelphia, Atlanta, and Boston suburbs, LQs are relatively high. In the Los Angeles (Orange County), Detroit, Pittsburgh, and St. Louis suburbs, they are roughly at the national norm, and among the remaining they are significantly lower. LQs for the remaining industry groups show considerable variation among the suburbs, although for the most part LQs for the two government industry groups are relatively low.

Taken as a whole, the suburbs must be regarded as diversified economies, much less narrowly specialized in any one, two, or three industries than are their respective central cities.

This observation is particularly applicable in considering the large, heterogeneous, other services industry group. Here LQs range from a low of .85 to a high of 1.19 (from 27.4 to 36.8 percent of total employment), indicating that suburban employment in this industry group, which includes business-related, social, repair, and personal services, is everywhere substantial but typically not as large as in central cities.

A Closer Look at the Four Largest Central Cities

Analysis of the employment data for the four largest cities utilizing more detailed industry data permits a fuller picture of these city economies (Table 2.2).[2]

Table 2.2 Percentage of Employment by Industry and Selected Subgroups, 1987

	New York		Chicago		Philadelphia		Los Angeles	
	Central City	Suburbs	Central City	Suburbs	Central City	Suburbs	Central City	Suburbs
Primary	0.30	1.21	0.45	1.17	0.18	1.08	0.95	1.54
Construction	3.38	5.87	3.85	5.86	2.45	5.95	3.85	5.90
Manufacturing	9.59	14.02	16.45	16.12	11.21	17.02	18.98	18.44
TCU	5.86	4.37	6.02	4.71	5.38	4.35	4.55	2.82
Wholesale	6.28	7.95	7.51	5.93	5.31	5.92	6.39	5.08
Retail	10.97	16.65	15.47	18.28	13.64	17.71	14.60	16.93
FIRE	14.68	7.92	9.68	6.85	9.51	8.06	8.83	11.42
Other services[a]	34.49	30.45	28.90	28.21	33.78	28.99	30.86	28.37
Business-related	13.38	9.90	10.38	9.53	8.75	9.57	10.99	12.04
Repair	0.93	1.31	1.18	1.58	1.05	1.22	1.53	1.33
Social	15.62	15.07	13.58	12.85	21.42	14.55	11.69	9.87
Consumer	3.79	3.84	3.35	3.84	2.36	3.07	6.65	5.12
Government	14.43	11.57	11.67	12.85	18.53	10.92	10.98	9.50
Federal, civilian	1.94	1.25	1.96	1.48	6.57	1.37	1.49	1.16
Military	0.49	0.50	0.56	3.02	2.25	1.81	0.95	1.43
State, local	12.01	9.82	9.14	8.34	9.71	7.74	8.45	6.92

[a] Business-related services include SICs 73, 81, 89; repair services, SICs 75, 76; social services, SICs 80, 82, 84, 86; consumer services, SICs 70, 72, 78, 79; administrative and auxiliary not shown.

Source: Data supplied by the Bureau of Economic Analysis. Subgroups of other services, shown in parentheses, estimated from County Business Patterns.

New York City

We observe that New York City is more heavily specialized in FIRE and other services than the other cities (i.e., has larger shares of employment) and is also heavily specialized in transportation, communication, and utilities (TCU) and wholesaling. Its manufacturing sector is relatively small.

Employment data for component industries provide additional detail:

1. In manufacturing, the apparel and printing-publishing segments (not shown) are clearly the principal industries; other types of manufacturing are relatively unimportant.
2. Within the other services category, business-related services (including legal) account for almost 14 percent of total employment, well in excess of the shares of the other cities, attesting to the major role that advanced services play in the New York City economy.
3. In TCU, the larger share of air transport services (not shown) provides evidence of New York's role as a national and international services center.
4. The relatively large share of communications employment (not shown) reflects in part New York's preeminent role in radio and TV broadcasting.
5. The relatively large role of state and local government would appear to be an indication that the public sector in the New York City government is larger than in other cities. It also reflects, no doubt, the considerable presence of state government offices within the city.

Finally, it must be noted that the measures fail to capture the importance of scale. Because larger market size strongly favors development of higher levels of specialization in many activities (e.g., law firms, consultants, advertising agencies), it is likely that share data significantly understate the extent of specialization and, accordingly, the importance of higher level specialists in the labor markets of large cities, especially New York.

Chicago

Chicago's role as a major distribution center with a well-developed financial sector and a continued heavy commitment to manufacturing is readily observed. A relatively large share of employment in trucking and warehousing (not shown) underlines the importance of goods distribution already noted in the large wholesaling sector. Manufacturing is characterized by relatively strong diversification (not shown), with relatively large shares of employment in commercial printing, meat products, fabricated metals (metal forgings and stampings), electrical equipment (communications equipment), and machinery excluding electrical (metal-working equipment). In assessing these measures, we must keep in mind that county data are being examined. Accordingly, the extensive manufacturing activities that lie outside the city's borders, but within Cook County, are included.

Philadelphia

Philadelphia's important role as a services center is due in large measure to its other services and government sectors, which together account for over half of all employment. Within the former, the employment share of social services (disproportionately health and educational services) is larger than in the other cities. Health services are of special importance, accounting for over 12 percent of all jobs and reflecting, in part, the presence of six major teaching hospitals. Government accounts for almost 19 percent of all jobs, compared to roughly 14 percent and 12 percent in New York and Chicago, the differences being the result of a larger military presence (e.g., U.S. naval shipyards) and a number of important civilian federal establishments (including one of the largest postal centers, a major immigration-naturalization center, and the headquarters of Conrail).

Financial services and wholesaling are less important in relative terms than in New York City and Chicago, whereas in TCU and retailing, Philadelphia falls into third and fourth place, respectively. In manufacturing and construction, Philadelphia ranks, respectively, third and fourth.

Los Angeles

Because Los Angeles County overbounds the city of Los Angeles so badly, Los Angeles County data probably do not fully reveal the extent of Los Angeles city's specialization in some activities. This may well be the case in FIRE, TCU, wholesaling, and business services. Nevertheless, Los Angeles seems to be significantly specialized in wholesaling, FIRE, and other services relative to the nation (see LQs in Table 2.1).

What is clear is that Los Angeles is relatively heavily committed to manufacturing. There is considerable diversification in this sector (not shown), with the strongest commitment to transportation equipment (aircraft and guided missiles), electrical and electronic equipment (radio and TV communication equipment and electronic components), apparel, and machinery (largely computers, industrial machinery, and construction equipment).

Specialization of the Other Ten Cities

Further insights into the economic specialization of individual cities may be gained by examining the LQs for the remaining ten cities (Table 2.1). If we examine simply the service categories other than retailing and government (i.e., TCU, wholesaling, FIRE, and other services), we observe that five of the ten (i.e., Atlanta, Boston, Dallas, Minneapolis, and St. Louis) are relatively heavily specialized as regional service centers with high concentrations (LQs above 1.10) in three or more of these industry groups.

Columbus (a state capital), with its heavy specialization in state-local employment (LQ 1.19), is a somewhat different type of regional center, with heavy specialization in FIRE (LQ 1.42), above-average employment in wholesaling and other services (LQs of 1.06 and 1.03), and the heaviest concentration of retailing employment of all the cities (LQ 1.15), in part because it is the headquarters for several retail and fast-food corporations.

Cincinnati and Detroit are cities with important manufacturing activities. Pittsburgh, an old manufacturing city now largely divested of this employment, shows relatively heavy concentration (1.31) only in the other services industry group (due in part to its hospitals and two large universities). Washington, D.C., as the nation's capital, is, of course, a major government center (LQ 11.21 in federal civilian employment). Its specialization in other services (LQ 1.38) suggests its importance as a location for a variety of business and consulting services and trade associations.

Changing Industrial Structure

Evidence of how cities and suburbs have changed in the 1970s and 1980s—how they are altering their relative specialization and what they seem to be becoming—is examined below.

Changes in the U.S. Economy

An essential first step is to examine changes that have occurred in the U.S. economy as a whole, for changes in city and suburb must be evaluated in light of what has been taking place on a broader scale throughout the U.S. economy.

Table 2.3 highlights national changes by presenting the distribution of U.S. employment among major industrial groups in 1969 and 1987. Briefly, we observe that there has been a major shift away from manufacturing and into service employment, with the greatest gains in FIRE and other services. There has also been some decline in the importance of TCU and government as a source of employment and gains in wholesaling, retailing, and construction.

Employment Increases and Decreases in Cities and Suburbs

In making comparisons among metropolitan areas and between central cities and suburbs, we look first at employment growth rates during the two periods and then at rates of job increase and job decrease. Job increases are simply net increases in employment in those industry groups that showed gains; job decreases are net decreases in those industry groups that showed losses. Annual rates of net overall employment change for 1969–1979 and 1979–1987 are shown in Table 2.4.

In general, suburban employment growth rates exceeded comparable rates for central cities by wide margins during both periods. This was not true, however, for Columbus during either period or for Minneapolis and Pittsburgh during the 1980s.

We observe further that several central cities lost employment during one or both periods: New York and Boston (first period only); Philadelphia, Detroit, and St. Louis (both periods); Pittsburgh (second period). Only in the Pittsburgh metropolitan area in the 1980s, however, were there employment losses in the suburbs.

Rates of job increase and job decrease (not annualized) provide a sense of the extent of the transformations that were taking place in some of the central cities (Table 2.5). Job decreases and job increases expressed as a percentage of total employment at the beginning of each period are shown in Table 2.6 for the eight central cities with the poorest employment growth experience during the 1970s.

Clearly, the 1970s was a period of difficult transformation for a number of the older cities of the U.S. economy, with job decreases in excess of 10 percent of initial employment in New York, Philadelphia, Boston, and St. Louis. The 1980s brought an improved performance for some but not for all. New York, Philadelphia, Boston, and Washington improved, but Detroit, Pittsburgh, and St. Louis appear to be in greater trouble. Chicago's position seems to have deteriorated marginally, at least according to these measures.

In the suburbs, job decreases were less than 5 percent in virtually all cases and in most cases were negligible (Table 2.5). Only in the Pittsburgh metropolitan area during the 1980s were suburban job decreases high (13 percent) relative to the central city.

Distribution of Job Increases and Job Decreases

Table 2.5, which distributes job increases and job decreases among industry groups, makes clear that manufacturing was the principal source

Table 2.3   Percentage Distribution of U.S. Nonfarm Employment, 1969, 1987, and Change in Industry Shares, 1969–1987

	1969	1987	Change
Agriculture service, forest, fishery, other	0.59	0.99	0.40
Mining	0.82	0.77	−0.05
Construction	5.22	5.50	0.28
Manufacturing	24.00	15.51	−8.49
TCU	5.59	4.85	−0.74
Wholesale	4.77	4.97	0.22
Retail	15.64	16.83	1.19
FIRE	5.50	7.95	2.45
Other services	19.07	26.74	7.67
Federal, civilian government	3.41	2.49	−0.92
Military	4.00	2.25	−1.75
State, local government	11.39	11.14	−0.25
	100.00	100.00	

Note: Other services include business-related services (SICs 73, 81, 89); repair services (SICs 75, 76); social services (SICs 80, 82, 84, 86); consumer services (SICs 70, 72, 78, 79).

Source: Data supplied by the Bureau of Economic Analysis.

Table 2.4   Annual Rates of Net Overall Employment Change, 1969–1979, 1979–1987

	1969–1979		1979–1987	
	Central City	Suburb	Central City	Suburb
New York	−1.3	2.2	1.2	2.9
Chicago	0.4	3.5	0.3	3.5
Philadelphia	−2.0	2.2	−0.2	2.8
Los Angeles	2.3	6.9	2.0	4.3
Atlanta	2.1	5.2	2.1	7.3
Boston	−0.3	2.1	1.6	3.0
Cincinnati	1.1	4.0	1.1	3.1
Columbus	2.6	2.3	2.7	1.0
Dallas	3.7	5.3	3.7	7.5
Detroit	−0.6	3.7	−1.6	2.5
Minneapolis	2.6	3.3	2.4	2.3
Pittsburgh	0.5	1.6	−0.2	−0.6
St. Louis	−0.8	2.6	−2.9	3.3
Washington	0.4	3.9	0.9	4.8
U.S.	2.2		1.9	

Source: Data supplied by the Bureau of Economic Analysis.

Table 2.5 Shares and Rates (not annualized) of Job Increase (JI) and Job Decrease (JD) by Industry, 1969–1979, 1979–1987

	U.S.		New York		Chicago		Philadelphia		Los Angeles	
	1969–79	1979–87	1969–79	1979–87	1969–79	1979–87	1969–79	1979–87	1969–79	1979–87
Cities										
Construction	6.2	5.1	(5.9)	9.3	(5.0)	1.5	(8.5)	(2.7)	2.4	5.3
Manufacturing	4.1	(94.4)	(49.1)	(66.5)	(80.7)	(91.7)	(51.9)	(65.2)	5.8	(96.6)
TCU	3.6	2.5	(9.8)	(18.8)	(7.4)	1.2	(5.0)	(16.8)	3.4	1.5
Wholesale	6.8	3.0	(8.8)	(9.2)	4.5	(1.5)	(8.9)	(4.6)	9.2	4.2
Retail	18.8	17.1	(15.1)	4.8	8.1	7.6	(13.1)	(0.1)	14.4	11.0
FIRE	11.1	13.5	(5.2)	21.2	19.8	13.1	(0.5)	7.8	12.6	14.0
Other services	31.4	49.6	93.5	53.9	45.8	72.1	43.2	71.8	41.5	58.0
Federal, civilian government	0.1	1.0	(3.5)	(3.1)	(2.5)	0.3	(8.3)	8.0	0.1	0.2
State, local government	14.7	4.3	4.2	10.5	21.0	(6.6)	56.3	(10.7)	9.2	2.6
All other: JI	3.1	4.0	2.3	0.3	0.8	2.2	0.6	12.4	1.4	3.1
JD	(100.00)	(5.6)	(2.6)	(2.4)	(4.5)	(0.3)	(3.9)	—	(100.00)	(3.4)
Rates: JI (+)	27.2	17.0	2.1	15.8	10.4	10.1	0.3	7.3	26.2	17.3
JD (−)	1.2	1.9	14.3	5.7	6.1	7.6	20.6	8.7	0.5	0.4
Suburbs										
Construction			(35.9)	11.5	5.7	5.7	3.6	7.1	7.1	5.2
Manufacturing			0.9	(73.1)	9.0	(100.00)	(20.6)	(91.6)	18.3	8.7
TCU			4.0	3.6	3.8	5.8	2.8	3.1	3.0	2.4
Wholesale			15.0	8.8	8.7	7.3	10.4	6.8	5.6	7.3
Retail			12.6	13.2	18.6	19.6	22.6	15.7	17.7	13.4
FIRE			12.0	12.6	11.2	8.0	13.3	14.1	12.3	16.5
Other services			41.6	47.4	30.0	47.4	35.0	50.3	27.3	41.6
Federal, civilian government			0.5	0.9	(19.6)	0.9	(3.3)	0.6	0.2	1.2
State, local government			11.4	(17.3)	11.5	1.3	10.8	(8.5)	7.0	2.0
All other: JI			1.1	2.0	1.3	3.9	1.5	2.4	1.5	1.9
JD			(64.1)	(9.5)	(80.4)	—	(76.1)	—	(100.00)	(100.00)
Rates: JI (+)			25.6	26.9	45.9	33.3	28.7	26.5	97.8	39.9
JD (−)			0.9	0.7	3.6	0.1	4.6	2.5	0.6	0.1

(continues)

Table 2.5 (Continued)

	Atlanta		Boston		Cincinnati		Columbus		Dallas	
	1969–79	1979–87	1969–79	1979–87	1969–79	1979–87	1969–79	1979–87	1969–79	1979–87
Cities										
Construction	(28.7)	5.5	(12.4)	4.9	0.3	4.1	0.4	4.0	5.6	3.2
Manufacturing	(42.8)	(39.3)	(18.1)	(72.8)	(64.4)	(98.8)	(58.3)	(88.3)	7.8	2.2
TCU	4.3	9.5	(7.3)	(2.4)	(12.9)	(1.1)	2.7	1.5	4.2	7.7
Wholesale	15.2	(59.5)	(17.4)	(12.9)	7.4	5.8	6.8	4.1	10.3	4.2
Retail	11.5	6.3	(23.2)	3.5	20.6	16.2	20.1	21.7	18.0	14.0
FIRE	12.1	13.7	(4.0)	25.8	11.1	12.8	11.8	19.5	12.5	19.4
Other services	30.0	58.9	71.6	57.2	45.2	59.2	36.1	42.0	25.4	40.7
Federal, civilian government	5.0	(1.2)	(7.1)	(10.3)	(16.4)	0.3	(6.7)	0.4	2.6	1.4
State, local government	21.2	2.9	28.4	8.2	14.4	0.3	21.2	4.7	9.2	3.8
All other: JI	0.6	4.4	—	0.5	1.0	1.5	1.0	2.2	4.5	3.3
JD	(28.5)	—	(10.5)	(1.6)	(6.3)	(0.1)	(35.0)	(11.7)	(100.00)	—
Rates: JI (+)	25.8	18.9	11.8	17.6	14.0	14.2	33.8	25.4	43.4	34.0
JD (−)	2.4	0.9	14.8	4.2	2.5	5.2	4.2	1.6	0.2	—
Suburbs										
Construction	7.4	9.4	(27.2)	10.9	9.5	3.9	5.4	7.4	9.8	7.4
Manufacturing	1.4	8.3	7.5	—	14.0	4.5	25.2	(99.6)	17.9	13.1
TCU	8.8	5.7	4.1	2.3	2.9	6.7	2.1	0.5	3.6	2.7
Wholesale	10.8	9.5	8.3	8.3	4.4	3.7	3.0	(0.3)	4.1	3.0
Retail	23.4	21.1	17.3	14.8	23.7	26.7	16.5	22.9	18.8	21.3
FIRE	11.5	9.9	10.5	12.1	7.8	4.0	11.3	10.4	6.3	10.7
Other services	24.0	26.4	37.0	49.0	25.1	40.3	24.5	50.0	18.5	29.8
Federal, civilian government	0.1	1.9	—	0.9	0.6	2.6	(79.8)	1.7	0.3	0.6
State, local government	12.6	4.7	14.3	(100.00)	10.8	4.7	10.0	4.5	18.2	8.0
All other: JI	0.1	3.0	0.9	1.8	1.2	3.0	1.9	2.5	2.5	3.4
JD	(100.00)	—	(72.8)	—	(100.0)	—	(20.2)	(0.1)	—	—
Rates: JI (+)	67.1	76.1	24.6	28.1	49.6	29.6	28.7	14.6	79.0	83.8
JD (−)	0.5	—	1.5	0.9	0.3	—	4.9	4.8	—	—

	Detroit 1969–79	Detroit 1979–87	Minneapolis 1969–79	Minneapolis 1979–87	Pittsburgh 1969–79	Pittsburgh 1979–87	St. Louis 1969–79	St. Louis 1979–87	Washington 1969–79	Washington 1979–87
Cities										
Construction	(10.5)	(2.0)	1.5	3.2	4.2	(2.4)	(1.1)	(1.0)	(10.7)	0.7
Manufacturing	(44.6)	(79.7)	7.7	(83.6)	(82.9)	(74.1)	(52.1)	(48.5)	(10.0)	1.4
TCU	(5.3)	(4.0)	3.3	5.2	(5.2)	(10.2)	(8.5)	(8.7)	(18.2)	(6.0)
Wholesale	(12.4)	(1.8)	7.5	3.0	3.4	(3.3)	(11.4)	(9.2)	(17.5)	(12.4)
Retail	(15.5)	(4.4)	14.8	14.6	21.0	8.7	(17.5)	(2.5)	(27.8)	4.0
FIRE	(6.8)	6.5	13.0	17.2	16.3	14.0	9.2	(2.8)	5.4	7.4
Other services	61.8	90.6	39.1	49.4	49.0	73.8	80.7	(20.5)	54.3	77.6
Federal, civilian government	(1.7)	(0.8)	(9.6)	1.4	1.3	(0.1)	(8.0)	(0.8)	28.7	(66.6)
State, local government	36.5	(7.2)	11.9	5.3	2.8	(9.1)	7.7	(5.5)	9.3	8.0
All other: JI	1.6	2.9	1.0	0.7	2.0	3.4	2.4	100.0	2.3	0.7
JD	(3.2)	(0.1)	(90.4)	(16.4)	(11.8)	(0.8)	(1.5)	(0.5)	(15.8)	(14.9)
Rates: JI (+)	3.1	2.8	30.2	20.9	9.6	11.2	3.7	0.5	10.4	11.9
JD (−)	9.3	14.6	0.7	0.1	4.7	13.1	11.4	22.2	6.7	4.6
Suburbs										
Construction	3.8	0.1	4.5	7.7	5.7	1.7	5.8	5.4	6.4	9.1
Manufacturing	3.2	2.5	7.9	5.2	(62.6)	(69.7)	1.5	2.1	3.6	4.2
TCU	2.8	2.0	1.6	(84.6)	5.4	(2.1)	5.6	3.6	3.6	6.4
Wholesale	9.1	3.6	6.4	1.0	7.7	9.3	9.0	3.5	5.5	4.5
Retail	25.8	17.6	25.5	18.4	21.9	10.4	23.7	16.7	17.6	16.2
FIRE	13.2	9.7	8.8	11.9	6.9	8.0	9.2	11.5	9.8	9.5
Other services	33.3	62.3	30.4	48.9	33.8	63.7	32.3	51.6	35.5	42.9
Federal, civilian government	(7.6)	0.6	0.2	0.1	0.6	0.1	(41.8)	1.2	5.8	1.8
State, local government	7.9	(100.0)	13.8	5.5	10.5	(11.4)	11.1	(100.0)	11.7	1.7
All other: JI	0.9	1.7	0.9	1.4	7.6	6.8	1.8	4.3	0.6	3.8
JD	(92.4)	—	(100.0)	(15.4)	(37.4)	(16.8)	(58.2)	—	(100.0)	—
Rates: JI (+)	44.9	23.2	39.9	20.8	19.0	8.4	30.3	30.6	52.2	46.5
JD (−)	4.8	0.4	0.4	0.1	1.8	13.2	0.5	0.4	4.4	—

Note: Other services include business-related services (SICs 73, 81, 89); repair services (SICs 75, 76); social services (SICs 80, 82, 84, 86); consumer services (SICs 70, 72, 78, 79). Shares of job increases are shown without parentheses; shares of job decreases, with parentheses. Job increases are the sum of all (net) gains in industry groups that have gained employment. Job decreases are the sum of all (net) losses in industry groups that have lost employment. Rates of JI (+) and JD (−) are shown as percentages of total employment at the beginning of the period.

Source: Data supplied by the Bureau of Economic Analysis.

Table 2.6   Job Increases (JI) and Job Decreases (JD) as a Percentage of Employment (not annualized) in Eight Central Cities, 1969–1979, 1980–1987

	1969–1979		1980–1987	
	JI	JD	JI	JD
New York	2.1	14.3	15.8	5.7
Chicago	10.4	6.1	10.1	7.6
Philadelphia	.3	20.6	7.3	8.7
Boston	11.8	14.8	17.6	4.2
Detroit	3.1	9.3	2.8	14.6
Pittsburgh	9.6	4.7	11.2	13.1
St. Louis	3.7	11.4	.5	22.2
Washington	10.4	6.7	11.9	4.6

Note: For explanation of job increases and job decreases, see Table 2.5.

Source: Data supplied by the Bureau of Economic Analysis.

of job decreases in those central cities where job decrease rates were high, although decreases in employment also occurred in a number of other industry groups in New York, Philadelphia, Boston, Detroit, and Pittsburgh in one or both periods. The job decreases due to manufacturing reflect the increasing competition from areas of lower labor costs as firms shifted production to the South and overseas. A number of suburbs, especially in the Pittsburgh metropolitan area, also lost manufacturing jobs, but here losses were less significant.

The other services industry group was the single largest source of employment expansion in every central city with the single exception of St. Louis city during the 1980s. The shares of job increases accounted for by other services were very large indeed, from 30 to 94 percent of all job gains in virtually every central city during both periods. Gains in FIRE were also substantial in most cities, accounting for well over one-tenth of all job increases in eight cities during the 1970s and ten cities during the 1980s.

Among the suburbs, manufacturing was typically a source of growth or, at least, of stability. Rates of employment increase in manufacturing were in almost every instance relatively modest, however, and, except for the metropolitan areas of Dallas (both periods) and Los Angeles, Cincinnati, and Columbus (first period), accounted for less than 10 percent of job increases in suburbs (Table 2.5). In addition, the suburbs were undergirded by large retailing sectors that grew more or less in pace with overall employment.

For suburbs, as for central cities, the other services industry group was the single largest contributor to employment expansion. Because employment increases occurred over a broader spectrum of industries in the suburbs, the shares of job increases accounted for by other services

Table 2.7 Number of Suburbs in Which Industry Growth Rates Exceeded Rates of Change in Total Employment, 1969–1979, 1979–1987 (N=14)

	1969–1979	1979–1987
Construction	8	10
Manufacturing	1	0
TCU	5	2
Wholesale	13	8
Retail	12	7
FIRE	14	13
Other services	14	14
Federal government	0	3
State, local government	5	0

Note: Other services include business-related services (SICs 73, 81, 89); repair services (SICs 75, 76); social services (SICs 80, 82, 84, 86); consumer services (SICs 70, 72, 78, 79).

Source: Data supplied by the Bureau of Economic Analysis.

were smaller but were, nevertheless, large: 30 percent or more in nine suburbs during the 1970s and in thirteen suburbs during the 1980s. Moreover, there were two other industrial categories, wholesaling and FIRE, that tended to grow at a faster rate than overall employment. This is clearly seen in the industry tallies of Table 2.7, which show the number of suburbs among those studied in which industry growth rates exceed the rate for total employment.

It is unfortunate that the BEA provides no industry breakdown of employment in the large other services category. It is particularly important to distinguish between business services and other more residentially oriented services. However, a breakdown (based on *County Business Patterns* data) of the shares of other services job gains and job losses in the central cities and suburbs of the New York, Chicago, and Philadelphia metropolitan areas for the 1970–1980 and 1980–1985 periods is shown in Table 2.8.

These estimates indicate that among the four subcategories of other services—business-related, repair, consumer, and social—business-related and social services were responsible for the major contributions to employment growth in all central cities and suburbs in the large other services category, with repair and consumer services accounting for much smaller shares.

Three findings stand out in examining the estimates of job increases in business-related and social services:

1. In general, in the suburbs shares of job increases within the other services grouping that were accounted for by business-related

Table 2.8 Job Increases (JI), Job Decreases (JD), and Shares (%) of JI Within Other Services, 1970–1980, 1980–1985

New York

	1970–1980		1980–1985	
	JI (+) JD (−)	JI Shares %	JI (+) JD (−)	JI Shares %
Central cities[a]				
Business-related	+46257	32.6	+60856	39.0
Repair	−2034		+306	0.2
Consumer	−33517		+7318	4.7
Social	+88862	62.6	+85650	54.9
Other	+6759	4.8	+1866	1.2
Total, other services	+141878 −35551	100.0	+155996	100.0
Suburbs[a]				
Business-related	+20892	30.5	+22382	43.3
Repair	+2443	3.6	+1871	3.6
Consumer	+3001	4.4	+4917	9.5
Social	+42125	61.5	+22530	43.6
Other	—	—	—	—
Total, other services	+68461	100.0	+51700	100.0

	Chicago				Philadelphia			
	1970–1980		1980–1985		1970–1980		1980–1985	
	JI (+) JD (−)	JI Shares (%)	JI (+) JD (−)	JI Shares (%)	JI (+) JD (−)	JI Shares (%)	JI (+) JD (−)	JI Shares (%)
Central cities[a]								
Business-related	+54850	32.1	+41533	59.6	+7771	13.8	+8307	36.2
Repair	+3224	1.9	+1190	1.7	−604		+167	0.7
Consumer	+12133	7.1	−20919		−12858		+2937	12.8
Social	+98025	57.3	+23695	34.0	+48554	86.2	+11521	50.2
Other	+2809	1.6	+3306	4.7	—		—	
Total, other services	+171014	100.0	+69724 −20919	100.0	+56325 −13462	100.0	+22932	100.0
Suburbs[a]								
Business-related	+21250	32.7	+24167	47.3	+44205	37.9	+37811	44.3
Repair	+3289	5.1	+2852	5.6	+5696	4.9	+2469	2.9
Consumer	+6137	9.4	+4795	9.4	+8349	7.2	+3950	4.6
Social	+34285	52.8	+17929	35.1	+58344	50.0	+41096	48.2
Other	—		+1300	2.5	—		—	
Total, other services	+64961	100.0	+51043	100.0	+116594	100.0	+85326	100.0

[a] Includes administrative and auxiliary.

Note: Business-related services include SICs 73, 81, 89; repair services, SICs 75, 76; consumer services, SICs 70, 72, 78, 79; social services, SICs 80, 82, 84, 86; other, administrative and auxiliary for services. See notes to Table 2.5 for methods of calculating JI and JD.

Source: Estimated from U.S. Bureau of the Census, *County Business Patterns, 1970, 1980, 1985* (Washington, DC: GPO, 1970, 1980, 1985).

services were comparable to those in the central cities. Measured in actual numbers of job gains, increases in business-related service employment in the suburbs were quite large relative to central cities (see Table 2.8). In the Philadelphia metro, they were several times as large.

2. Business-related services increased in importance (i.e., as a share of job increases in other services) in both cities and suburbs during the second period.

3. Within the social services group, health services accounted for a major share of job gains in both central cities and suburbs during both periods (not shown in Table 2.8). It is clear that the expansion of health services has played an important role in the growth of the suburbs, accounting for from 30 to 41 percent of job increases in other services in the suburbs of these three large metropolitan areas during the 1970s and from 20 to 30 percent during the 1980s.

Summary

The principal findings of the present chapter are threefold: First, employment in the suburbs has typically grown much more rapidly than in central cities, where in many cases heavy losses have been sustained, largely in the manufacturing sector. Second, employment gains in central cities have tended to focus on FIRE and other services, whereas gains in the suburbs have taken place over a broader front. Nevertheless, suburban employment gains have also been substantial in FIRE and other services, with strong growth also evinced in many places in retailing, wholesaling, and construction. Manufacturing, though not an important source of growth in jobs in most suburbs in recent years has, nevertheless, tended to provide stability. Third, analysis of three large metropolitan areas indicates that *within* the other services category, business-related services have nevertheless made important contributions to growth in both central cities and suburbs. Among the social services in both cities and suburbs, health services were a major source of job growth during both periods.

Notes

1. For evidence of the acceleration principle as it operates in construction employment in metropolitan economies, see Thomas M. Stanback, Jr., and Richard V. Knight, *The Metropolitan Economy* (New York, NY: Columbia University Press, 1970), pp. 65–67, 179–84.

2. These brief profiles rely not only on the measures shown in Table 2.2 but also on data not shown and on general knowledge.

3

Earnings Levels

Thus far, discussion has focussed on employment—on the numbers of workers employed in the several industry groups and how these numbers have changed. No attention has been given to earnings levels within city and suburban economies.

Earnings measures provide valuable insights into how city and suburban economies are faring. Within a given central city or suburb, relatively high earnings levels in an industry reflect the joint effects of some combination of higher skill levels, greater sheltering of workers through unions and credentialing, greater use of full-time employees, or the employment of fewer young workers, women, or minorities than is found in low-earnings industries. An increase in the share of jobs accounted for by industries with high average earnings implies an availability of more jobs for better-qualified workers. Conversely, an increase in the share accounted for by low-earnings industries implies a relatively greater availability of jobs for those with lower skills, education, and experience.

Earnings averages are, of course, crude indicators. They tell us nothing about the occupational mix of an industry. Firms in which earnings are relatively low may make heavy use of relatively poorly paid white-collar workers rather than blue-collar workers, and their growth will offer few job opportunities for persons who are only qualified for menial labor.

Nevertheless, earnings levels are a useful indicator and shed considerable light on the way in which changes in cities and suburbs are affecting job opportunities for various groups in the labor force.

Variations in Earnings Among Industries

Table 3.1 presents indices of the average earnings in several industry groups in the U.S. economy in 1969 and 1987. The earnings are expressed as multiples (i.e., ratios) of the average earnings in all industries combined. We note a wide variation in average earnings per worker among industries

Table 3.1   Indices of Average Earnings for U.S. Industry Groups, 1969, 1987

	1969	1987
Construction	1.29	1.20
Manufacturing	1.20	1.34
TCU	1.29	1.44
Wholesale	1.28	1.30
Retail	0.71	0.58
FIRE	1.03	0.91
Other services	0.83	0.91
Federal, civilian government	1.26	1.33
State, local government	0.88	1.00
All industries	1.00	1.00

Note: Average earnings in industry groups are expressed as a ratio to average earnings in all industries combined. Other services include business-related services (SICs 73, 81, 89); repair services (SICs 75, 76); social services (SICs 80, 82, 84, 86); consumer services (SICs 70, 72, 78, 79).

Source: Data supplied by the Bureau of Economic Analysis.

for 1987—from 1.44 (1.44 percent of the national average) for TCU to .58 for retailing. For the most part, the relative levels of the various industries in 1987 do not differ greatly from those of 1969. TCU, construction, manufacturing, wholesaling, and federal government are the five highest in both 1969 and 1987; state and local government, other services, FIRE, and retailing, the lowest. Retailing is by far the lowest in both years.

In some industries indices rise from 1969 to 1987; in others they fall, perhaps indicating a change in the mix of the industries the groups comprise or changes in employment and hiring practices. For example, the sharp decline in retailing is, doubtless, the result of several factors, including a disproportionate growth in the low-paying food-and-drink subsector of retailing, the increased employment of youth and women, and increases in part-time employment, all of which have characterized retailing as a whole more than any other industrial sector.

Central City–Suburb Comparisons of Industry Earnings

Table 3.2 presents industry indices of average earnings in 1987 for the fourteen central cities and suburbs. For both cities and suburbs, indices have been computed in the form of ratios of the average earnings per worker in the given industry to average earnings per worker for the city's total work force. Accordingly, the index for a given industry in the suburb can be compared directly with the index of the same industry in the central city to determine whether earnings levels are higher or lower.

Comparisons Among Industries. When central cities are compared, several observations may be made that are of interest for the analysis to follow:

1. Except in New York City, earnings in manufacturing are relatively high, 1.11 to 1.68.
2. Earnings levels vary most sharply among central cities in the FIRE industry group. Indices are relatively high in five cities: New York (1.52), Chicago (1.15), Philadelphia (1.17), Atlanta (1.11), and Boston (1.31). In the remainder of the fourteen central cities, indices are below 1.00. Each of the cities with a high FIRE earnings index is also relatively specialized in FIRE as measured by the location quotient indices of employment concentration in Table 2.1 (LQs are: New York, 1.85; Chicago, 1.22; Philadelphia, 1.20; Atlanta, 1.30; and Boston, 1.84). The two types of measures viewed together tell us much about these central cities: They are financial centers with heavy concentrations of FIRE workers with, on average, relatively high levels of earnings due, at least in part, to high-salaried executives and professionals. On the other hand, three of the central cities have high LQs in FIRE (Columbus, 1.42; Dallas, 1.54; and Minneapolis, 1.29) but low indices of earnings (.93, .93, and .99, respectively). Here, apparently, the specialization is of a different sort, with a smaller proportion of well-paid people (relative to the city's average), indicating a greater emphasis on processing—of credit cards, insurance policies, and the like.
3. The large and rapidly growing other services group is characterized everywhere by somewhat lower average earnings, with indices ranging from .98 to .75.
4. In construction, TCU, and wholesaling, average earnings are relatively high in virtually every central city. Only in Washington is the index for construction below 1.09, and in nine cities indices are 1.21 or above. TCU indices are 1.24 or above in all places; wholesaling indices range from 1.14 to 1.38 and federal government indices from 1.06 to 1.25, except in New York City (.96).
5. State-local government earnings levels are relatively low in most central cities, .97 or below in nine of them, no higher than 1.04 in the remaining five.
6. Retailing stands in a class by itself. It is an industry in which earnings are, on average, quite low. Among the fourteen cities, no index is above .62.

City and Suburban Earnings Compared. Average earnings for all industries combined are higher for central cities than for their suburbs

Table 3.2 Indices of Average Earnings by Industry, Central Cities (C) and Suburbs (S), 1987

1987	New York		Chicago		Philadelphia		Los Angeles/ Orange		Atlanta	
	C	S	C	S	C	S	C	S	C	S
Construction	1.16	0.99	1.34	1.23	1.24	1.17	1.26	1.22	1.09	0.88
Manufacturing	0.93	1.05	1.19	1.15	1.18	1.27	1.15	1.17	1.19	1.08
TCU[a]	1.24	0.98	1.34	1.21	1.45	—	1.34	1.19	1.46	1.33
Wholesale trade	1.17	1.00	1.25	1.17	1.24	1.20	1.19	1.13	1.28	1.21
Retail trade	0.53	0.48	0.56	0.49	0.53	0.53	0.60	0.57	0.60	0.51
FIRE	1.52	0.64	1.15	0.65	1.17	0.71	0.98	0.73	1.11	0.61
Other services	0.91	0.71	0.92	0.80	0.95	0.80	0.98	0.86	0.88	0.74
Federal, civilian government	0.96	0.92	1.15	1.03	1.12	1.14	1.16	1.01	1.18	1.00
State, local government	0.90	0.89	0.95	0.80	1.04	0.90	1.04	0.96	0.90	0.77
Total	1.00	0.78	1.00	0.85	1.00	0.89	1.00	0.90	1.00	0.82

	Columbus		Dallas		Detroit		Minneapolis		Pittsburgh	
	C	S	C	S	C	S	C	S	C	S
Construction	1.21	0.96	1.23	0.91	1.09	1.11	1.36	1.24	1.30	1.06
Manufacturing	1.46	1.48	1.23	1.09	1.68	1.37	1.34	1.44	1.56	1.27
TCU[a]	1.45	1.20	1.35	1.08	1.29	—	1.48	1.24	1.35	1.13
Wholesale trade	1.36	1.15	1.30	1.15	1.14	1.25	1.38	1.22	1.26	1.04
Retail trade	0.62	0.49	0.62	0.46	0.46	0.46	0.56	0.47	0.51	0.48
FIRE	0.93	0.57	0.93	0.44	0.83	0.56	0.99	0.71	0.91	0.49
Other services	0.91	0.69	0.91	0.72	0.75	0.81	0.84	0.68	0.95	0.75
Federal, civilian government	1.35	1.49	1.15	1.08	1.06	0.94	1.23	1.25	1.25	1.11
State, local government	1.03	0.91	0.90	0.77	0.90	0.84	0.97	1.02	1.01	0.89
Total	1.00	0.92	1.00	0.75	1.00	0.90	1.00	0.92	1.00	0.85

1987	Boston		Cincinnati	
	C	S	C	S
Construction	1.25	0.82	1.06	0.96
Manufacturing	1.11	0.99	1.52	1.25
TCU[a]	1.31	0.80	1.36	1.20
Wholesale trade	1.17	0.85	1.31	1.05
Retail trade	0.55	0.40	0.54	0.47
FIRE	1.31	0.37	0.80	0.44
Other services	0.93	0.62	0.82	0.66
Federal, civilian government	1.10	0.90	1.29	0.91
State, local government	0.93	0.65	0.92	0.82
Total	1.00	0.67	1.00	0.77

1987	St. Louis		Washington		Tally[b]		
	C	S	C	S	C>S	C=S	S>C
Construction	1.26	1.16	0.90	0.94	12	—	2
Manufacturing	1.31	1.37	1.23	1.06	8	—	6
TCU[a]	1.49	1.17	1.26	1.16	12	—	—
Wholesale trade	1.17	1.26	1.17	1.15	12	—	2
Retail trade	0.54	0.48	0.49	0.51	11	2	1
FIRE	0.95	0.67	0.90	0.56	14	—	—
Other services	0.84	0.71	0.98	0.81	13	—	3
Federal, civilian government	1.16	1.03	1.18	1.11	11	—	1
State, local government	0.90	0.84	1.00	0.80	12	1	—
Total	1.00	0.86	1.00	0.81	14	—	—

[a] TCU data not available for two suburbs.
[b] Where differences are ± .01, city and suburb scored as equal.

Note: Average earnings in industry groups are expressed as a ratio to average earnings in all industries in the central city. Other services include business-related services (SICs 73, 81, 89); repair services (SICs 75, 76); social services (SICs 80, 82, 84, 86); consumer services (SICs 70, 72, 78, 79).

Source: Data supplied by the Bureau of Economic Analysis.

Table 3.3   Earnings Indices for Subgroups of Other Services, 1987

	New York		Chicago		Philadelphia	
	Central City	Suburb	Central City	Suburb	Central City	Suburb
Business-related	1.00	.78	.99	.94	1.05	.92
Repair	0.66	.67	.82	.81	0.76	.79
Social	0.72	.77	.80	.72	0.88	.71
Consumer	0.76	.47	.52	.47	0.63	.47

Note: Average earnings for all industries in central city equals 1.00. Business-related services include SICs 73, 81, 89; repair services, SICs 75, 76; social services, SICs 80, 82, 84, 86; consumer services, SICs 70, 72, 78, 79.

Source: Estimated from U.S. Bureau of the Census, *County Business Patterns, 1970, 1980, 1985* (Washington, DC: GPO, 1987).

in all comparisons (Table 3.2). This does not mean, however, that suburban earnings are low in all industries. In manufacturing, suburban average earnings are higher than comparable earnings in the city in six of the fourteen metropolitan areas. Moreover, average earnings in construction, TCU, and wholesaling are well above overall city average earnings levels (though typically below city levels for these industries) in a number of suburbs. Among the remaining industry categories, retailing, FIRE, state-local government, and federal civilian employment, suburban earnings are for the most part relatively low.

Some additional light is shed by earnings estimates from *County Business Patterns* for four subgroups (business, repair, social, and consumer services) within the broad other services category in three of the largest metropolitan areas (see Table 3.3).

A considerable range in earnings indices within the other services group in each of these central cities and suburbs is observed.[1] Business-related services is the highest everywhere. This industry category comprises a considerable range of services including the well-paid legal-services industry and a number of fairly high-earnings professional-type services (e.g., accountants), along with a large number of relatively low-paid services (e.g., janitorial and security contract services). The large social services category (which includes health and education services) and repair services are somewhat below business-related services; and consumer services, which include personal services, hotels, and amusements, are lowest except in New York City.

In most comparisons, central city earnings are higher than suburban. Perhaps the most interesting observation here is that in the New York metropolitan area there is a large difference between city and suburban earnings in the business-related services, but in the social services suburban earnings are higher.

Why Average Earnings in Central Cities
Are Higher Than in Suburbs

That city earnings levels are typically higher than suburban levels is hardly surprising because the cost of living is higher in the city, reflecting higher rents, costs inherent in congestion, greater need for public services, and so on. Workers must earn more to live in the city and commuters must earn more to justify the time and costs of traveling daily into and out of the city.

But there are other possible reasons that aggregate and specific industry-level earnings are higher in the central city. One is that the city's economy may be more specialized in the sense of producing an array of more highly value-added goods and services (principally the latter) and in the process must make use of relatively more workers from the higher-paying occupational ranks (i.e., managers, professionals, and technicians). Another is that work arrangements and the labor force drawn upon by the suburban employer may make for lower average earnings. To the extent that the suburban firm makes greater use of part-time labor, average earnings per worker will, *ceteris paribus*, be lower, as will be the case if the firm is able to draw more readily upon (and use productively) youth or women, who typically command lower wage rates than adult males.

One indication that the differences between central city and suburban earnings are not simply a reflection of cost-of-living differences is to be found in the ratios of central city to suburban earnings computed for individual industries. If the cost of living were the only factor at work, the relationships between central city and suburban earnings and, accordingly, their ratios would be more or less the same among industries.

That this is far from the case is evident from inspection of the ratios of city to suburban earnings in each industry for the four largest metropolitan areas in a given year (e.g., 1987) (Table 3.4).

We note that in each metropolitan area ratios vary significantly among industries. The ratios are particularly high for FIRE. Apparently, the marked difference in city and suburban earnings of this industry reflects a significant difference in mix of activities between suburbs and cities, with suburban firms engaged principally in routine operations associated with serving residents or back-office activities, whereas central city operations include a heavier mix of high value-added functions.

The Trends in the Ratios of City to Suburban Earnings

City earnings levels are not only higher than those in the suburbs but the ratio of city to suburban average earnings (all industries combined)

Table 3.4 Average City Earnings as a Ratio of Average Suburban Earnings, Selected Industry Groups and All Industries, 1969, 1979, 1987

	Construction			Manufacturing			TCU		
	1969	1979	1987	1969	1979	1987	1969	1979	1987
New York	1.03	1.05	1.17	0.92	0.90	0.89	1.16	1.25	1.26
Chicago	1.97	1.04	1.09	1.06	1.06	1.03	1.06	1.08	1.10
Philadelphia	1.10	1.10	1.06	0.92	0.93	0.93	1.03	1.23	—
Los Angeles	0.99	1.01	1.04	0.95	1.04	0.99	1.18	1.19	1.13
Atlanta	1.10	1.14	1.23	0.98	1.12	1.11	1.13	1.18	1.10
Boston	1.45	1.52	1.52	1.14	1.14	1.12	1.24	1.59	1.64
Cincinnati	1.12	1.04	1.10	1.23	1.17	1.22	1.04	1.09	1.14
Columbus	1.16	1.19	1.26	1.11	1.09	0.99	1.06	1.26	1.21
Dallas	1.30	1.19	1.35	1.33	1.23	1.13	1.26	1.25	1.26
Detroit	1.03	0.99	0.98	1.05	1.14	1.23	1.01	1.03	—
Minneapolis	0.99	1.05	1.09	1.00	0.97	0.93	1.04	1.11	1.20
Pittsburgh	1.12	1.17	1.22	1.16	1.22	1.23	1.09	1.17	1.19
St. Louis	1.10	1.09	1.09	0.94	0.95	0.95	1.10	1.15	1.28
Washington	1.00	1.11	0.96	1.21	1.26	1.16	1.08	1.17	1.09

	FIRE			Other Services			Federal, Civilian		
	1969	1979	1987	1969	1979	1987	1969	1979	1987
New York	1.26	1.62	2.37	1.11	1.21	1.28	1.05	1.05	1.04
Chicago	1.18	1.44	1.77	1.24	1.17	1.16	1.02	1.16	1.12
Philadelphia	1.08	1.33	1.66	1.01	1.09	1.18	1.02	0.94	0.98
Los Angeles	1.17	1.18	1.35	1.15	1.09	1.14	1.14	1.12	1.14
Atlanta	1.36	1.63	1.82	1.00	1.11	1.19	1.34	1.25	1.19
Boston	1.59	2.30	3.55	1.27	1.47	1.51	1.15	1.13	1.23
Cincinnati	1.38	1.66	1.82	1.25	1.23	1.25	1.39	1.37	1.43
Columbus	1.27	1.45	1.62	1.21	1.33	1.32	1.01	0.97	0.91
Dallas	1.28	1.74	2.14	1.35	1.30	1.26	1.17	1.12	1.06
Detroit	1.13	1.23	1.49	0.85	0.91	0.92	1.07	1.03	1.12
Minneapolis	1.04	1.17	1.39	1.10	1.15	1.24	0.79	0.96	0.99
Pittsburgh	1.19	1.32	1.85	1.30	1.17	1.27	1.13	1.09	1.14
St. Louis	1.03	1.21	1.43	1.08	0.99	1.18	1.20	1.26	1.13
Washington	1.33	1.51	1.60	1.15	1.22	1.20	0.99	1.02	1.07

	Wholesale			Retail		
	1969	1979	1987	1969	1979	1987
New York	1.12	1.20	1.17	1.09	1.13	1.10
Chicago	1.08	1.05	1.07	1.07	1.12	1.14
Philadelphia	1.04	1.07	1.04	0.98	1.07	1.01
Los Angeles	1.19	1.12	1.06	1.04	1.08	1.06
Atlanta	1.07	1.09	1.06	1.03	1.15	1.19
Boston	1.38	1.47	1.37	1.40	1.42	1.37
Cincinnati	1.24	1.26	1.24	1.10	1.11	1.15
Columbus	1.09	1.25	1.18	1.31	1.17	1.27
Dallas	1.50	1.21	1.13	1.08	1.17	1.34
Detroit	1.01	0.97	0.91	1.02	1.06	1.01
Minneapolis	1.08	1.11	1.13	1.17	1.12	1.20
Pittsburgh	1.09	1.11	1.21	1.06	1.04	1.07
St. Louis	0.91	0.84	0.93	1.06	1.02	1.12
Washington	1.22	1.12	1.02	1.01	1.03	0.95

	State, Local			All Industries		
	1969	1979	1987	1969	1979	1987
New York	1.07	1.14	1.01	1.10	1.19	1.28
Chicago	1.22	1.27	1.19	1.14	1.15	1.17
Philadelphia	1.36	1.24	1.16	1.04	1.09	1.12
Los Angeles	1.03	1.09	1.09	1.08	1.10	1.12
Atlanta	1.24	1.20	1.16	1.09	1.20	1.23
Boston	1.49	1.58	1.42	1.33	1.45	1.49
Cincinnati	1.18	1.11	1.12	1.29	1.27	1.31
Columbus	1.25	1.13	1.14	1.14	1.09	1.08
Dallas	1.18	1.21	1.17	1.34	1.33	1.33
Detroit	1.10	1.13	1.07	1.01	1.12	1.11
Minneapolis	1.10	1.03	0.95	1.04	1.06	1.09
Pittsburgh	1.12	1.13	1.13	1.13	1.11	1.18
St. Louis	1.23	1.08	1.08	1.06	1.06	1.16
Washington	0.97	1.32	1.25	1.17	1.27	1.23

(continues)

Table 3.4 (Continued) Changes in Ratios, City/Suburb Ratios[a]

	1969–1987			1969–1979			1979–1987		
	+	NC	–	+	NC	–	+	NC	–
Construction	9	1	4	8	2	4	9	3	2
Manufacturing	4	3	7	5	4	5	2	5	7
TCU[b]	8	2	2	12	2	0	7	1	4
Wholesale	5	5	4	8	—	6	4	—	10
Retail	8	3	3	9	1	4	8	—	6
FIRE	14	—	—	13	1	—	14	—	—
Other services	9	2	3	8	—	6	9	3	2
Federal, civilian	6	3	5	4	1	9	8	1	5
State, local	2	2	10	7	1	6	—	5	9
Total	12	1	1	8	3	3	10	3	1

[a] Where ratios in two years compared are equal or differ by .01 the comparison is scored as "no change" (NC).
[b] Data not available for two cities in TCU in 1987.

Source: Data supplied by the Bureau of Economic Analysis.

rose in most metropolitan areas from 1969 to 1987: twelve increases, one decrease, and one instance of no change (insignificant change) (Table 3.4).[2]

The finding that ratios of city earnings to suburban earnings have tended to rise over time is intriguing. One might have expected the opposite to be the case. The fact that suburbs have shown sustained growth over a long period suggests that there has been considerable opportunity for import substitution and for the addition of more complex and higher value-added activities to result in a narrowing, rather than a widening, of the city-suburb gap in average earnings.

Comparison of city-suburban earnings ratios in 1987 and 1969 at the industry level indicates that the tendency for central city earnings to rise disproportionately was much stronger in some industries than in others (Table 3.4). In FIRE, the city-suburban ratios rose in all fourteen metropolitan areas, but among the remaining industry groups it was only in construction, TCU, retail, and other services that ratios increased in as many as eight central cities. In state and local government, ratios declined in ten central cities and in manufacturing, in seven.

When changes in the ratios are compared, we find that the ratios increased during both periods in all areas in FIRE (although in Los Angeles during the first period the increase was small and scored as "no change") and in construction, retailing, and other services in a majority of metropolitan areas. In manufacturing, TCU, wholesaling, and state-local employment, however, the ratios increased in a smaller number of central cities (decreased in a larger number) in the second period, suggesting a relative strengthening of the suburban economies.

Evidence of Upgrading
in the City and Suburban Economies

In order to shed further light on the tendency for central city earnings levels to rise relative to suburban levels, ratios of average earnings of both central cities and suburbs to the national average in 1969 and 1987 have been computed. Among the cities, a majority showed increases in ratios, whereas among the suburbs, a minority showed increases (Table 3.5).

It is interesting to observe which cities showed increases in ratios and which did not. The nine that showed increases include not only New York, Chicago, Philadelphia, and Los Angeles but also Atlanta, Boston, Dallas, and St. Louis—all cities found previously to be relatively heavily specialized as national or regional service centers—plus Wash-ington, D.C., which has over the past decade or so has become increasingly important as a service center as well as the seat of the federal government (see Chapter 2). Among the two remaining cities identified as regional

Table 3.5 Ratios of Average Earnings in Central Cities and Suburbs to U.S. Average
Earnings, 1969, 1987

| | Central Cities | | | Suburbs | | |
	1969	1987	Change	1969	1987	Change
New York	1.23	1.44	+	1.11	1.12	=
Chicago	1.19	1.22	+	1.04	1.04	=
Philadelphia	1.08	1.18	+	1.04	1.05	=
Los Angeles	1.21	1.23	+	1.12	1.10	−
Atlanta	1.02	1.20	+	0.94	0.98	+
Boston	1.10	1.31	+	0.82	0.88	+
Cincinnati	1.10	1.08	−	0.85	0.82	−
Columbus	1.05	0.97	−	0.92	0.90	−
Dallas	1.05	1.18	+	0.78	0.89	+
Detroit	1.30	1.31	=	1.29	1.18	−
Minneapolis	1.11	1.11	=	1.07	1.02	−
Pittsburgh	1.11	1.08	−	0.98	0.92	−
St. Louis	1.09	1.17	+	1.03	1.01	−
Washington	1.24	1.38	+	1.06	1.12	+
Tally						
+			9			4
=			2			3
−			3			7

Source: Data supplied by the Bureau of Economic Analysis.

centers in Chapter 2, Columbus showed a decline in ratios; Minneapolis
showed no change.

Among the suburbs, it is again instructive to examine increases or
decreases in ratios for individual places. The four that showed an increase
were the burgeoning suburbs of Atlanta, Boston, Dallas, and Washington.
In the suburbs of three of the four largest metropolitan areas—New
York, Chicago, and Philadelphia—there were no significant changes in
ratios, whereas the ratio declined slightly in the Los Angeles surrogate
suburban county (Orange).

Some additional evidence is gained by examining ratios in 1969 and
1987 for industry groups in central cities and suburbs (Table 3.6). Tallies
of 1969–1987 changes in ratios are shown in Table 3.7.

In most central cities and suburbs, average earnings in manufacturing
and wholesaling have risen relative to the United States, suggesting that
in the face of sharper competition, firms in these larger metropolitan
areas have tended to become engaged in more highly value-added and
specialized activities. In TCU and FIRE, most central cities have been
upgrading, whereas most suburbs have not (FIRE earnings declined
relative to the nation in eleven of the fourteen suburbs) (Table 3.7). The

Table 3.6 Ratios of Average Earnings in Central Cities and Suburbs to U.S. Average Earnings by Industry, 1969, 1987

	Construction		Manufacturing		TCU		Wholesale		Retail	
	1969	1987	1969	1987	1969	1987	1969	1987	1969	1987
Central cities										
New York	1.19	1.38	1.03	1.00	1.17	1.23	1.19	1.30	1.17	1.30
Chicago	1.31	1.35	1.08	1.08	1.11	1.13	1.14	1.18	1.12	1.16
Philadelphia	1.12	1.22	1.00	1.04	1.03	1.18	1.04	1.13	1.00	1.08
Los Angeles	1.22	1.29	1.15	1.05	1.12	1.14	1.13	1.13	1.21	1.27
Atlanta	0.89	1.08	0.93	1.07	1.03	1.21	1.06	1.19	1.05	1.24
Boston	1.11	1.36	0.95	1.08	1.03	1.19	1.07	1.17	1.02	1.23
Cincinnati	1.08	0.95	1.11	1.22	1.05	1.01	1.03	1.08	1.02	0.99
Columbus	1.05	0.97	1.07	1.06	1.01	0.97	1.01	1.01	1.18	1.03
Dallas	0.99	1.20	1.03	1.09	1.02	1.11	1.03	1.18	1.04	1.26
Detroit	1.36	1.19	1.42	1.64	1.12	1.17	1.19	1.15	1.17	1.04
Minneapolis	1.21	1.25	1.09	1.11	1.06	1.15	1.15	1.18	1.12	1.08
Pittsburgh	1.18	1.17	1.18	1.26	1.06	1.02	1.02	1.05	0.99	0.95
St. Louis	1.18	1.23	1.05	1.14	1.08	1.21	1.03	1.06	1.07	1.08
Washington	0.93	1.04	1.17	1.26	1.01	1.21	1.21	1.24	1.10	1.15
	1969	1987	1969	1987	1969	1987	1969	1987	1969	1987
Suburbs										
New York	1.16	1.18	1.12	1.13	1.01	0.98	1.07	1.11	1.08	1.18
Chicago	1.23	1.25	1.03	1.05	1.05	1.02	1.06	1.10	1.05	1.02
Philadelphia	1.02	1.14	1.09	1.12	1.00	—	1.00	1.09	1.02	1.06
Los Angeles	1.23	1.24	1.20	1.07	0.95	1.01	0.94	1.07	1.17	1.19
Atlanta	0.81	0.88	0.95	0.96	0.91	1.11	0.99	1.12	1.02	1.05
Boston	0.77	0.89	0.83	0.97	0.83	0.73	0.78	0.86	0.73	0.90
Cincinnati	0.96	0.86	0.91	1.00	1.01	0.89	0.83	0.87	0.92	0.86
Columbus	0.91	0.77	0.96	1.07	0.95	0.81	0.92	0.86	0.90	0.81
Dallas	0.76	0.89	0.77	0.96	0.81	0.88	0.69	1.05	0.96	0.94
Detroit	1.33	1.21	1.35	1.34	1.10	—	1.18	1.27	1.15	1.03
Minneapolis	1.23	1.15	1.09	1.19	1.02	0.95	1.06	1.04	0.96	0.90
Pittsburgh	1.06	0.95	1.01	1.03	0.97	0.85	0.94	0.87	0.94	.089
St. Louis	1.07	1.13	1.12	1.20	0.98	0.95	1.13	1.13	1.01	0.96
Washington	0.93	1.07	0.96	1.09	0.93	1.11	1.00	1.22	1.09	1.21

(continues)

Table 3.6 (Continued)

	FIRE		Other Services		Federal, Civilian		State, Local		All Industries	
	1969	1987	1969	1987	1969	1987	1969	1987	1969	1987
Central cities										
New York	1.42	2.40	1.35	1.43	1.01	1.04	1.30	1.30	1.23	1.44
Chicago	1.19	1.54	1.28	1.23	0.97	1.05	1.16	1.16	1.19	1.22
Philadelphia	1.10	1.53	1.05	1.23	1.00	0.99	1.35	1.23	1.08	1.18
Los Angeles	1.08	1.33	1.34	1.32	1.04	1.06	1.37	1.27	1.21	1.23
Atlanta	1.06	1.47	0.93	1.16	1.12	1.07	1.02	1.08	1.02	1.20
Boston	1.21	1.88	1.20	1.34	1.01	1.08	1.32	1.22	1.10	1.31
Cincinnati	1.00	0.95	1.00	0.97	1.07	1.04	1.02	0.99	1.10	1.08
Columbus	0.91	0.99	1.05	0.97	1.03	0.98	1.01	1.00	1.05	0.97
Dallas	1.00	1.22	1.02	1.18	1.04	1.02	1.00	1.06	1.05	1.18
Detroit	1.06	1.20	1.12	1.08	1.02	1.04	1.30	1.18	1.30	1.31
Minneapolis	1.05	1.21	1.06	1.02	0.84	1.03	1.23	1.08	1.11	1.11
Pittsburgh	1.05	1.08	1.11	1.13	1.03	1.02	0.98	1.09	1.11	1.08
St. Louis	0.97	1.23	0.97	1.07	1.07	1.02	1.13	1.06	1.09	1.17
Washington	1.05	1.37	1.37	1.48	1.24	1.22	1.04	1.38	1.24	1.38
Suburbs										
New York	1.12	1.01	1.22	1.12	0.96	1.00	1.21	1.28	1.11	1.12
Chicago	1.01	0.87	1.03	1.06	0.95	0.94	0.95	0.98	1.04	1.04
Philadelphia	1.02	0.92	1.04	1.04	0.98	1.01	0.99	1.06	1.04	1.05
Los Angeles	0.92	0.98	1.17	1.15	0.92	0.93	1.32	1.17	1.12	1.10
Atlanta	0.78	0.80	0.92	0.97	0.84	0.90	0.83	0.93	0.94	0.98
Boston	0.76	0.53	0.94	0.89	0.88	0.88	0.88	0.85	0.82	0.88
Cincinnati	0.72	0.52	0.80	0.78	0.77	0.73	0.86	0.88	0.85	0.82
Columbus	0.72	0.61	0.87	0.74	1.02	1.08	0.81	0.88	0.92	0.90
Dallas	0.78	0.57	0.76	0.94	0.89	0.96	0.85	0.91	0.78	0.89
Detroit	0.94	0.81	1.32	1.16	0.96	0.93	1.18	1.10	1.29	1.18
Minneapolis	1.01	0.87	0.96	0.82	1.06	1.04	1.12	1.13	1.07	1.02
Pittsburgh	0.88	0.59	0.85	0.89	0.92	0.90	0.88	0.96	0.98	0.92
St. Louis	0.94	0.86	0.90	0.91	0.89	0.91	0.92	0.98	1.03	1.01
Washington	0.79	0.85	1.19	1.23	1.26	1.15	1.07	1.10	1.06	1.12

Source: Data supplied by the Bureau of Economic Analysis.

evidence is less clear in the heterogeneous other services group, although ratios have risen in more cities than suburbs.

These findings must be interpreted in light of two reservations. The first is that in three metropolitan areas the ratio may have been affected by significant increases in the cost of living arising out of rapid growth. In Atlanta, Dallas, and Washington, there were increases in virtually every industry category in *both* central city and suburb, indicating that increases in earnings were strongly influenced by general increases in wage levels as well as by changes at the industry level. The second is that skill transformation need not always be reflected in higher earnings. Greater specialization and higher productivity may in some instances be brought about by rearrangement of work, redefinition of tasks (and retraining), and application of newer technology without commensurate increases in wages and salaries.

Nevertheless, there is evidence here that central cities—at least those that have played roles as national or regional service centers—have shown a greater tendency toward upgrading relative to the nation than have their suburbs.

Evidence from the Commuter Data

The Distribution of City Earnings: Evidence from the "Journey to Work" Data

The importance of commuters to the city must be seen in terms of the wages and salaries they receive as well as their numbers. The earnings of these workers were relatively high compared with those of residents working in the city in 1980. In New York, they were almost double the wages of resident city workers; in Chicago, 52 percent higher; in Philadelphia, 69 percent higher; and in Los Angeles, 47 percent higher (Table 3.8). In only two of the fourteen cities were in-commuter wages less than 20 percent higher then the average of those residents who worked in the city.

Because "Journey to Work" data only provide average earnings for all resident workers, we can only speculate how large a number of residents earn wages and salaries that are, on average, as high as those paid to in-commuters. Nevertheless, such a speculation can be useful in providing some sense of how wages and salaries are distributed among city resident workers.

The following hypothetical example, suggesting the magnitudes that may well be involved, uses as an example New York City in 1980, with all numbers drawn from "Journey to Work" data.

Table 3.7 Number of Cities and Suburbs in Which Ratios of Average Earnings to U.S. Average Earnings Increased (+), Decreased (−), or Showed No Change (NC), 1969–1987

	Central City			Suburbs		
	+	NC	−	+	NC	−
Construction	10	1	3	8	1	5
Manufacturing	10	2	2	11	2	1
TCU[a]	11	0	3	4	0	8
Wholesale	11	2	1	10	1	3
Retail	7	2	5	6	0	8
FIRE	13	0	1	3	0	11
Other services	8	0	6	5	2	7
Federal government	6	2	6	6	3	5
State, local government	4	3	7	10	1	3
Total	9	2	3	4	3	7

[a] Data not available for TCU in two suburbs.

Note: Other services include business-related services (SICs 73, 81, 89); repair services (SICs 75, 76); social services (SICs 80, 82, 84, 86); consumer services (SICs 70, 72, 78, 79).

Source: Based on Table 3.6.

Table 3.8 Average Earnings of In-Commuters as a Percentage of Average Earnings of Residents Working in Central City, 1980

Central City	Percentage
New York	190
Chicago	152
Philadelphia	169
Los Angeles	147
Atlanta	120
Boston	165
Cincinnati	115
Columbus	126
Dallas	126
Detroit	150
Minneapolis	115
Pittsburgh	126
St. Louis	167
Washington	142

Source: Data supplied by the Bureau of Economic Analysis.

Commuters account for about one-fifth of the workers in the city of New York and are relatively highly paid ($24,645 in 1980, 90 percent above resident worker levels ($12,955). It would not seem unreasonable to suppose that among residents working in the central city at least another one-fifth of the city work force earn, on average, wages as high as the commuters. The best evidence of this is found in employment data by occupation for *residents* of central city and suburbs. Table 3.9 presents distributions of city and suburban residents among occupations for the four largest metropolitan areas. In 1986 roughly one-fourth of all central city residents were employed as managers, executives, or professionals, occupations that should pay wages at least as high as received by the average commuter. In addition, there are surely a sizable number of residents among several of the other occupations (e.g., technicians, administrative support) who are employed in well-paying positions.

Because commuters, who account for about 20 percent of the work force in New York City, account for about 32 percent of total wages, the two groups of well-paid workers combined would account for about 40 percent of the work force and about 64 percent of total earnings. The remaining residents, accounting for 60 percent of those employed, would be paid the remaining 36 percent of the total wages of $49,773 million earned in the city and receive an average wage of only $8,837— scarcely more than one-third of the average wage of the well-paid groups!

Of course, the above is but one possible scenario, but it underscores a basic observation: that large city economies are labor markets within which there is a sharp wage dichotomy—a large group of resident workers holds jobs in which wages are only a fraction of those paid the remainder.

A second point is simply that the trend toward a larger share of the cities' jobs being filled by commuters (noted in Chapter 1) suggests a trend toward a larger share of well-paying jobs—jobs with occupational requirements that cannot be met by the cities' unskilled and poorly educated.[3]

Some additional detail is provided for the year 1980 by commuter and resident-worker employment data for industry groups. In virtually every city, resident workers hold the largest share of jobs in state-local government (Table 3.10), presumably because local government jobs are more readily accessible to residents than to outsiders. Among the remaining industry groups, the shares of employment held by residents are typically highest in other services and "trade" (combined wholesale and retail).[4] Shares are smallest in construction and TCU—industries in which average wages for the city work force tend to be high (Table 3.2).

Rankings of average wages of resident workers in the various industry groups are also presented in Table 3.10, with average rankings for the ten central cities shown for each industry. We observe that wages are typically lowest in trade, followed by other services and state-local government—the same industries in which residents find jobs most

Table 3.9 Percentage Distribution of City and Suburban Resident Workers by Occupation, 1983, 1986

	New York City			Chicago			Philadelphia			Los Angeles		
	1983	1986	Change	1983	1986	Change	1983	1986	Change	1983	1986	Change
Executive, manager	11.7	13.3	+	9.1	9.7	+	8.4	9.6	+	12.6	13.1	+
Professional	13.9	15.8	+	13.0	13.5	+	12.5	14.5	+	13.8	13.4	–
Technician	2.1	2.2	+	–	–		–	–		3.3	3.2	–
Sales	10.3	9.9	–	9.2	10.0	+	11.7	9.3	–	11.1	11.3	+
Administrative support	23.1	21.8	–	20.4	20.9	+	23.6	20.4	–	19.8	18.4	–
Service occupation	16.6	15.7	–	14.5	14.0	–	15.1	16.3	+	11.8	11.3	–
Craft	8.3	8.5	+	10.7	11.2	+	10.0	10.0	=	11.0	12.3	+
Machine operator	7.0	5.9	–	10.4	8.4	–	7.8	6.5	–	8.3	8.9	+
Transport operator	3.5	3.6	+	4.2	3.9	–	–	–		3.2	3.4	+
Laborers	3.1	2.9	–	5.4	5.8	+	–	–		3.6	3.5	–

	New York Suburbs			Nassau/Suffolk			Chicago Suburbs			Philadelphia Suburbs			Anaheim		
	1983	1986	Change	1983	1986	Change	1983	1986	Change	1983	1986	Change	1983	1986	Change
Executive, manager	17.2	16.9	–	13.3	15.1	+	14.2	15.2	+	12.4	14.0	+	16.7	15.0	–
Professional	17.2	19.3	+	15.8	15.1	–	16.1	13.7	–	14.7	14.9	+	13.5	11.2	–
Technician	3.0	2.8	–	–	–		–	–		–	–		–	–	
Sales	14.1	13.3	–	13.3	14.1	+	15.7	14.3	–	12.3	13.0	+	15.1	15.1	=
Administrative support	17.9	17.7	–	19.1	19.4	+	17.4	19.4	+	17.3	17.8	+	17.2	16.7	–
Service occupation	10.9	11.2	+	13.1	11.6	–	10.2	10.5	+	12.1	10.9	–	11.4	13.5	+
Craft	9.5	8.7	–	11.1	12.1	+	10.8	11.0	+	12.2	12.3	+	12.1	11.1	–
Machine operator	2.9	3.6	+	3.9	3.3	–	5.5	5.4	–	7.4	5.5	–	5.8	6.3	+
Transport operator	2.7	3.1	+	–	–		2.9	2.9	=	–	–		–	–	
Laborers	3.0	2.6	–	–	–		3.4	3.9	+	–	–		–	–	

Source: U.S. Bureau of the Census, Current Population Reports, series P-23, no. 159, Population Profile of Employment and Unemployment, 1989 (Washington, DC: GPO, 1989).

readily. The industries in which average resident wages are highest—TCU, construction, federal-civilian, and manufacturing—are all industries in which residents' shares of the work force for the most part rank poorly.

The ratios of average in-commuter wages to average resident worker wages (city work force) for industry groups provide additional insights. We observe that, on average, the differentials are greatest (i.e., ratios are highest) in the relatively lower-wage trade and other services categories, least in the two government categories.

The findings for FIRE are somewhat different. In some cities (New York, Chicago, Philadelphia, Boston, St. Louis), ratios of in-commuter to resident wages are relatively high; in other cities (especially Atlanta, Cincinnati, Columbus, Dallas, Minneapolis), ratios are well below overall levels.

In-Commuters to the Suburbs

The commuter data available from the Bureau of Economic Analysis for the suburbs do not disclose information on earnings, but they do provide estimates of the numbers of in-commuters to the suburbs. These data, shown for 1960 and 1980 in Table 1.6, indicate that in virtually every suburb the percentage of the suburban work forces accounted for by in-commuters rose sharply from 1960 to 1980.

Here is indirect but important evidence that the growing suburban economies are opening up a sizable number of jobs attractive enough to draw an increasing number of workers from outside metropolitan boundaries. It also goes far to explain the disproportionate rise in suburban employment relative to suburban population observed earlier (see Table 1.2).

Conclusions

The findings in this chapter add considerably to our picture of the kinds of transformations that are taking place in central city and suburb. As central cities have become more narrowly focussed in terms of specialization in services, especially in TCU, FIRE, and other services, they have tended to upgrade in terms of average earnings paid, indicating employment of higher proportions of skilled and better-educated workers. Such upgrading has been made possible through increased employment of in-commuters. The data for commuter employment and wages clearly show that these workers drawn from outside the central city are disproportionately well paid relative to resident city workers. Moreover,

Table 3.10 Selected Employment and Wage Measures, Resident Workers and In-Commuters, Central Cities, 1979

Resident Workers as Percentage of City Work Force

	New York	Chicago	Philadelphia	Los Angeles	Atlanta	Boston	Cincinnati	Columbus
Construction	71.3	77.6	52.8	84.1	32.3	27.6	63.2	77.8
Manufacturing	78.7	84.6	70.4	88.2	36.2	43.3	63.4	81.6
TCU	68.8	79.8	52.9	85.9	31.2	31.8	56.5	80.9
Trade	82.0	87.9	71.4	91.3	43.0	49.4	76.1	89.1
FIRE	77.3	87.0	58.7	92.5	41.6	35.3	72.9	89.6
Other services	82.4	89.1	69.6	93.5	48.7	46.2	80.7	91.7
Federal, civil government	82.3	88.7	60.0	89.7	42.3	40.3	71.2	85.2
State, local government	82.3	93.1	86.3	91.7	51.4	54.9	90.9	91.7
All industries	79.6	86.7	67.9	90.5	42.0	44.4	72.6	87.6

Average Wages, Residents Working in City, Ranked from Highest to Lowest Average Wage

	New York	Chicago	Philadelphia	Los Angeles	Atlanta	Boston	Cincinnati	Columbus
Construction	5	1	4	2	5	4	3	3
Manufacturing	7	3	5	5	4	6	2	4
TCU	1	2	1	1	3	1	1	1
Trade	8	8	8	8	8	8	8	8
FIRE	3	6	6	4	1	5	5	5
Other services	6	7	7	7	6	7	7	7
Federal, civil government	2	4	2	3	2	2	4	2
State, local government	4	5	3	6	7	4	6	6

Ratio of Average Wages, In-Commuter, to Average Wages, Residents in City Work Force

	New York	Chicago	Philadelphia	Los Angeles	Atlanta	Boston	Cincinnati	Columbus
Construction	1.64	1.31	1.65	1.28	1.26	1.55	1.04	1.09
Manufacturing	2.32	1.47	1.78	1.52	1.18	1.72	1.01	1.13
TCU	1.57	1.30	1.43	1.29	1.27	1.47	1.10	1.19
Trade	2.19	1.72	1.97	1.69	1.32	1.91	1.24	1.35
FIRE	1.99	1.62	1.90	1.34	0.91	1.66	0.92	1.01
Other services	1.83	1.55	1.79	1.29	1.06	1.70	1.05	1.19
Federal, civil government	1.42	1.41	1.34	1.33	1.22	1.41	1.07	1.21
State, local government	1.49	1.16	1.24	1.39	1.18	1.33	1.09	1.23
All industries	1.90	1.52	1.69	1.47	1.20	1.65	1.15	1.26

Resident Workers as Percentage of City Work Force

	Dallas	Detroit	Minneapolis	Pittsburgh	St. Louis	Washington	Average Rank
Construction	77.4	63.6	62.5	79.7	23.7	28.5	6.4
Manufacturing	72.6	72.4	65.0	73.7	29.9	28.7	5.8
TCU	70.6	72.4	60.4	77.7	21.0	26.5	7.4
Trade	83.5	78.7	78.3	89.4	39.5	43.2	3.4
FIRE	85.5	76.1	79.8	90.1	30.5	32.7	4.1
Other services	86.3	78.9	79.2	89.8	45.2	42.1	2.2
Federal, civil government	75.9	82.3	64.4	87.2	31.7	29.6	5.1
State, local government	87.5	86.3	78.9	91.3	63.4	48.5	1.3
All industries	80.2	76.9	73.2	84.3	36.7	35.4	

Average Wages, Residents Working in City, Ranked from Highest to Lowest Average Wage

	Dallas	Detroit	Minneapolis	Pittsburgh	St. Louis	Washington	Average Rank
Construction	5	2	1	3	1	7	3.3
Manufacturing	3	1	3	1	4	2	3.6
TCU	2	3	2	2	2	4	1.9
Trade	6	8	8	8	8	8	7.9
FIRE	4	6	5	5	6	3	4.6
Other service	8	7	7	7	7	6	6.9
Federal, civil government	1	5	4	4	3	1	2.4
State, local government	7	4	6	6	5	5	5.3

Ratio of Average Wages, In-Commuter, to Average Wages, Residents in City Work Force

	Dallas	Detroit	Minneapolis	Pittsburgh	St. Louis	Washington	Average Ratio
Construction	1.14	1.23	1.02	1.06	1.30	1.47	1.28
Manufacturing	1.22	1.29	0.99	1.05	1.54	1.25	1.35
TCU	1.23	1.24	1.13	1.17	1.41	1.42	1.30
Trade	1.34	2.01	1.29	1.27	1.97	1.72	1.63
FIRE	1.12	1.53	1.03	1.13	1.71	1.29	1.35
Other services	1.22	1.82	1.10	1.26	1.76	1.42	1.43
Federal, civil government	1.10	1.36	1.10	1.07	1.37	1.30	1.27
State, local government	1.15	1.26	1.12	1.13	1.26	1.32	1.23
All industries	1.26	1.50	1.15	1.26	1.67	1.42	1.42

Note: Other services include business-related services (SICs 73, 81, 89); repair services (SICs 75, 76); social services (SICs 80, 82, 84, 86); consumer services (SICs 70, 72, 78, 79).

Source: Data based on 1980 "Journey to Work" tabulations supplied by the Bureau of Economic Analysis.

they find employment disproportionately in those sectors of the city's economy in which average earnings are highest.

On the other hand, as the more rapidly growing suburbs have matured and broadened their economies, different patterns of earnings have emerged. Although earnings levels have been upgraded relative to the nation in manufacturing, wholesaling, and state-local government, the suburbs have tended to specialize in low-paying back-office or residentiary financial activities. In the larger, heterogeneous other services category, which has gained everywhere in employment terms, there is evidence that certain of the business services have flourished with earnings levels not greatly below those that obtain in the central city. Social services, consumer services, and retailing have grown apace, but city-suburban earnings differentials remain significantly large in most metropolitan areas.

Notes

1. Indices are ratios of average first-quarter earnings in industry to average first-quarter earnings in total central city county (counties) excluding government.

2. "No change" is defined as less than or equal to + or −.01.

3. There is evidence that, at least in some central cities, this increase was due in part to out-migration from the city. Matthew Drennan analyzed residence adjustment data from New York City by borough and found that when Manhattan was examined separately, the out-flow of commuter earnings was approximately the same percentage of resident worker earnings in 1987 as in 1969 (about 67 percent), although the comparable percentage for the five boroughs combined had risen significantly. The relative increase in out-flow of earnings (i.e., in the residence adjustment) was the result of an out-migration of residents of the other four boroughs to the suburbs. No longer counted as residents of the city, they were defined at the end of the period as commuters and their earnings as commuter earnings. Matthew P. Drennan, "The Local Economy," pp. 7–38, in Charles Brecher and Raymond D. Horton, eds., *Setting Municipal Priorities, 1990* (New York, NY: New York University Press, 1989).

4. "Trade" is a one-digit industry classification that combines retail and wholesale. Average earnings in trade are quite low because low earnings in the large retail sector outweigh the effect of relatively high earnings in the much smaller wholesale sector.

4

Agglomeration Economies and the Development of Cities and Suburbs

In the present chapter, attention focuses on the importance of agglomeration economies, how central cities and suburbs have been altered to accommodate changes in industrial specialization, and, within the suburbs, the importance of new agglomerations in providing employment in the key business-related, FIRE, and social services industries. The significance of these new agglomerations within the suburbs for the continuing vitality of the central city is then assessed.

The Importance of Agglomeration Economies

The location of firms is not random but rather is determined by the relative advantages and disadvantages perceived to exist in alternative locations. Firms will accept additional costs—usually reflected in higher rents, higher labor costs, higher taxes—in order to take advantage of the special benefits a particular location affords.

Many of the benefits a location can provide derive from agglomeration, or the clustering together of firms. By locating near other firms, a business can receive several special advantages. One obvious advantage is easy and speedy access to individuals in other firms with whom there are frequent interactions. These frequent patterns of interchange underlie the clustering of different financial institutions, brokerage houses, and legal firms in the central business district and also link the corporate headquarters, advertising agencies, accounting firms, and legal firms that cluster in the midtown areas of large cities.

Another benefit of agglomeration is the marketing advantage it affords. By concentrating in one location, firms make it easier for clients to locate and utilize their services. In retailing, this benefit has long been recognized in the form of shopping centers, but it is also evident in the concentration of advertising agencies, legal services, and financial institutions in Manhattan.

A third benefit of agglomeration is the savings it allows through the sharing of major capital investments and infrastructure. The mass transit systems and large airports that can exist only in large and densely settled metropolitan areas are examples. Similarly, only in large settlements can major cultural facilities such as museums, art galleries, and theaters be supported. Thus, there are substantial social savings and cultural benefits associated with agglomeration.

A fourth benefit resulting from agglomeration—and perhaps the most important—is the development of easy access to a specialized labor force. Only a large concentration of firms will attract a pool of expertise such as freelance editors, media consultants, and other specialized workers. One firm, or even a small number of firms, could not provide a sufficient market for such specialists, but together a larger number of firms can. Similarly, only a large work force provides the underpinning for specialized educational institutions and other training facilities that enhance the quality of the local labor supply. Thus, in each of these ways—the interchange of information, the ease of marketing, the efficient use of infrastructure, and the gathering of a diverse labor force—agglomeration provides benefits that a single firm in isolation could not obtain at any price.[1]

Agglomeration Economies
and Central City Development

As the U.S. economy has moved rapidly from a goods-oriented to a services-oriented economy, a variety of producer services—finance, wholesaling, insurance, consulting, advertising, engineering, and the like—have risen sharply in importance. The focal point of these activities is the metropolitan economy and within the metropolitan economy the central city itself. It is here that agglomeration economies have played their greatest role and communication and access among firms is maximized.

The changing economic role of these cities has been accompanied by dramatic physical transformations. In describing the results of these transformations in the typical large city of today, Bernard J. Frieden writes:

> The manufacturing districts of the 1950s, the busy harborside warehouses, the freight terminals, some of the once-thriving department stores and specialty shops, and most working-class neighborhoods are no more. Gone, too, are the rubble fields of the 1960s, where the wrecking crews had cleared land for urban renewal, but the builders were nowhere in sight. The new centers feature a cluster of office towers mixed with new hotels

and civic buildings, freeways pumping heavy traffic to the edge of downtown, modern housing complexes, one or more shopping malls, some
renovated office buildings and warehouses, many new restaurants . . .[2]

Frieden observes major growth and change in five areas:[3]

1. New office complexes. Since 1960, the thirty largest cities have
   added as much downtown office space as they had accumulated
   in all the preceding years.
2. New hotels. From 1960 through the early 1980s, the thirty-eight
   largest metropolitan areas added more than 300 downtown hotels
   with 110,000 rooms. "In addition to providing lodgings for visitors,
   many of the new hotels built flashy atriums and dazzling public
   spaces that enhanced the glitter of downtown."
3. Downtown shopping malls. More than 100 downtown shopping
   malls have opened since 1970, most of them "distinctly urban"
   specialty centers (such as Fanueil Hall Market in Boston) or large
   mixed-use centers (e.g., Walter Tower Place in Chicago).
4. Convention centers. More than 100 cities have built convention
   centers in the past twenty years. These centers have added significantly to the cities' economic bases, generating many billions
   annually in local spending.
5. Gentrification. Since the 1970s, there has been a significant increase
   in interest in city living among young professionals. This so-called
   gentrification has brought with it both a restoration of run-down
   historic neighborhoods and a new demand for upper-income con-
   dominiums and cooperatives, while encouraging expansion of museums and the construction of theaters and stadiums.

Not mentioned but clearly of major importance has been the increase
in highways, intra-urban transportation systems, and airport facilities.
Even today, forty years after the initiation of the interstate highway
system, a number of cities continue to improve access through additions
or expansions to major arteries. A number of places, including Atlanta,
San Francisco, and Washington, D.C., have put in place or expanded
rail systems linking the center city with outlying areas, including in
some instances suburban destinations, and most large metropolitan areas
have built or expanded airport facilities.

All these changes and others have served to increase the attractiveness
of the city as a place in which to do business, through improving and
expanding the physical infrastructure, enriching amenities, and extending
access. All four of the benefits of agglomeration mentioned earlier are

enhanced as the cities have been transformed to accommodate the requirements of the new service economy.

Agglomeration Economies and Suburban Development

The importance of agglomeration economies to suburban development is not as readily recognized as in the case of the central cities. Yet there is considerable evidence that economic growth in the suburbs is increasingly focussed on a restricted number of magnet areas in which locational advantages associated with agglomeration play a key role.

The Rise of Suburban Centers

In a recent monograph and journal article, two urban geographers, Truman A. Hartshorn and Peter O. Muller, examined the growth of suburban centers, "suburban downtowns," which they describe as "one of the most important developments in the 200-year-plus urban history of the United States."[4] In the introduction to their monograph, the authors state:

During the past two decades, as the nation's postindustrial economy and society emerged and began to mature, American metropolitan regions experienced a profound transformation in their structural and functional organization. The industrial-era metropolis, characterized by a dominant central-city core and a girdling ring of residential suburbs, turned inside out and split asunder in this period. With surprising speed in the 1970s and 80s, suburbs have evolved from a loosely-organized "bedroom community" into a full-fledged "outer city," characterized by metropolitan-level employment and activity concentrations and functional shifts that amount to nothing less than the achievement of suburban economic, social, and geographic independence from the nearby central city that spawned these satellite settlements several decades ago.

The suburbs have led the way in new job formation in both traditional blue and white collar occupations and in new high technology occupations, the latter of which became almost exclusively suburban in nature by the mid-1980s. Indeed, suburban employment now exceeds central city totals in a large share of major metropolitan area labor markets.[5]

In examining the development of suburban downtowns, Hartshorn and Muller identify four stages with approximate dates as follows: Stage I—Bedroom Community (pre-1960); Stage II—Independence (1960–1970); Stage III—Catalytic Growth (1970–1980); and Stage IV—High Rise/High Technology (1980–present). Whereas Stage I is self-explanatory, the remaining stages require brief explanation.[6]

At the forefront of Stage II was the success of the regional shopping centers, as retailers recognized the importance of the growing suburban market and began to serve it directly. At the same time, there was a rapid development of industrial parks adjacent to the new highway and freeway corridors, catering to light industry and distribution/warehouse operations, as well as office parks that were similarly located. The latter initially attracted small sales offices but soon became popular with large corporations as sites for regional sales offices.

Stage III was marked by an intensification of suburban growth as the suburbs pulled ahead of the central cities in total employment. During these years, development took place in a number of different types of centers: *suburban freeway corridors*, dominated by linear belts of high-rise office structures and hotels; *retail-strip corridors* along major suburban arterial highways and, in some cases, specialized research-and-development, high-technology corridors (e.g., Boston's Route 128 beltway); *regional mall centers*, with rings of office buildings encircling large shopping centers; *diversified office centers*, originated by developers as office parks and rapidly expanded thereafter; *large-scale mixed-use centers*, providing retail, office, and hotel facilities, usually within an integrated "new town" complex (typically master-planned by a single developer); *old town centers*, with new growth grafted onto a preexisting suburban town (e.g., Bethesda, Maryland); and *suburban specialty centers*, developed around an airport, medical center, sports complex, university complex, or military installation (e.g., the O'Hare Airport commercial center).

Stage IV represents further development in which prestigious high-rise buildings with decked parking structures appear and sufficient scale is attained to attract commercial tenants at rents equal to or above those in the central business district. At this stage, high-tech corridors also appear with significant numbers of small firms clustered about. In addition, it is also common to find upscale housing development of various types, including townhouses and high-rise units.

The Hartshorn-Muller study is based primarily on a careful analysis of six suburban downtowns (two each in three major metropolitan areas), along with some limited references to a number of other suburbs, also based on field visits. Two of the metropolitan areas studied, Atlanta and Philadelphia, are among those analyzed in this study; the third is Houston.

In the Atlanta metropolitan area, the two suburban centers studied, Cumberland/Galleria and Perimeter Center–Georgia 400, accounted for 38,726 and 55,726, jobs respectively. In *each* of these centers, office space exceeds that of the Atlanta central business district (14 and 16 million square feet versus 13 million within the central business district). In addition, a third center, Lenox-Buckhead, accounts for 9 million square feet.[7] The distribution of 1985 employment in the two centers is shown in Table 4.1.

In treating the Philadelphia metropolitan area, Hartshorn and Muller demonstrate at the outset that suburban development has been especially rapid, with employment growth outstripping that of the central city since the beginning of the 1950s. Development in the two suburban centers studied, King of Prussia and Cherry Hill, is clearly far advanced. At King of Prussia, development began in the mid-1950s when a number of major manufacturers established facilities there, followed in the early 1960s by a shopping mall, which became a major shopping complex including John Wanamaker, Gimbles, and J. C. Penney. During the late 1960s and the 1970s, industrial parks and office complexes grew rapidly: The American Baptist Convention headquarters and a top-name theater were established, and a variety of cabarets, cinemas, and restaurants; numerous mid-rise apartments; and three additional leading department stores were added. The 1980s saw the construction of a $17 million convention center (132,000 square feet and one of the ten largest in the nation) adjacent to the new high-rise Sheraton Hotel. In addition, high-tech activity has expanded nearby to form a complex, "Silicon Gulch," which in 1985 accounted for over 9,000 jobs.

Rapid employment growth began at Cherry Hill in 1961 with the establishment of a large regional shopping center. Growth followed quickly through the establishment of light industry and the addition of a major RCA facility. The 1970s brought diversified white-collar growth as office parks expanded and hotel facilities flourished to serve Cherry Hill's Garden State Race Track horse-racing market.

The Cervero Study

In a more recent study Robert Cervero has examined fifty-seven suburban centers throughout the United States with at least 1 million square feet of office floor space, 2,000 or more workers, and a location at least 5 radial miles from the regional CBD. Though not descriptive in terms of historical development the study examined evidence relating to a variety of characteristics: scale and location, employment, density and design, composition of land use, nature of land ownership, work force travel, and site-and areawide transportation, services, and conditions. Centers were classified into six groups: office parks, office and concentration centers, large-scale mixed-use developments, moderate scale mixed-use developments, subcities, and large-scale office growth corridors.

Table 4.1 Percentage Distribution of Employment in Two Suburban Centers, 1987

	Cumberland/ Galleria	Perimeter Center–Georgia 400
Retail	25	25
Services	25	20
FIRE	19	19
Wholesale	17	13
Other	14	23
Total	100	100

Source: Truman A. Hartshorn and Peter O. Muller, *Suburban Business Centers: Employment Expectations*, Final Report for U.S. Department of Commerce, EDA (Washington, DC: Department of Commerce, November 1986).

Table 4.2 presents for each group information relating to the size, location relative to CBD, and employment. One is struck by both the physical size of these centers and the relatively heavy proportions of management, administrative, and technical personnel employed, especially in office parks, office concentrations, moderate mixed-use developments, and subcities.

The Hartshorn-Muller and Cervero Studies as Evidence of Agglomeration Economies

Both Hartshorn-Muller and Cervero's studies make clear that these large agglomerations have attracted a variety of retailers, business service firms, and corporate offices. The studies also demonstrate that the attractiveness of these centers rests on close linkages to the suburban highway network, which makes it possible to draw upon a large pool of suburban and, to some extent, city workers, while offering ready access to the rich suburban market and a variety of business customers.

For firms locating in these "suburban downtown" areas there are important urbanization economies: Each firm profits by the presence of the other. Corporate offices can more readily receive visiting executives, salespeople, and customers because of attractive hotel and restaurant facilities; retail customers gain opportunities to shop a variety of stores; stores, in turn, gain from the heavier traffic that large retail agglomerations make possible; and workers of all types are provided opportunities to shop during lunch and after work or to lunch with friends away from the company dining hall. If firms are able to operate at lower costs because of lower rents, taxes, land costs, or wage rates, then the advantages of the suburban locations are, accordingly, increased.

Table 4.2 Comparison of Size, Location, and Employment Among Types of 57 Suburban Centers

	Office Park	Office Concentrations	Large Mixed-Use Developments	Moderate Mixed-Use Developments	Sub-cities	Office Growth Corridors
Size						
Acreage	549.1	2,593.0	7,813.0	697.4	1,223.3	120,530.0
Floor space[a]	2.97	5.69	12.29	3.77	12.72	26.48
Location						
Miles from CBD	18.0	15.4	20.4	13.0	15.7	25.0
Employment						
Total, average[b]	8.14	12.91	27.47	7.49	33.56	236.91
Average %						
Management	10.0	17.1	11.1	20.7	18.7	8.8
Administrative	20.3	15.9	12.3	15.3	13.9	8.9
Technical	39.1	22.5	15.2	15.5	18.6	19.4

[a] Millions of square feet in office-commercial-industrial uses.
[b] Full-time work force in thousands.

Note: Data are for 1985–1987.

Source: Adapted from Robert Cervero, *America's Suburban Centers: The Land Use–Transportation Link*, pp. 106–107, Table 5.1 and Figure 5.1. Used by kind permission of Unwin Hyman Ltd. © Robert Cervero, 1989.

Table 4.3 Employment/Population Ratios (E/Ps) and Residence Adjustment Percentages, Candidate Magnet Counties and Other Counties, 1969, 1979, 1987

	E/P			Residence Adjustment		
	1969	1979	1987	1969	1979	1987
New York						
Westchester	.42	.49	.59	35	26	28
Nassau	.38	.49	.60	43	35	25
Bergen	.41	.54	.67	31	16	11
Other[a]		.22–.38	.30–.47	57–139	53–198	40–193
Chicago						
Du Page	.31	.44	.58	100	63	29
Other[a]		.33–.49	.32–.49	19–47	22–68	32–81
Philadelphia						
Montgomery	.51	.62	.73	8	0.1	−5
Camden		.42	.50	26	18	12
Other[a]		.34–.47	.38–.53	27–66	32–51	27–54
Boston						
Middlesex	.45	.50	.70	7	0.6	−7
Norfolk	.37	.48	.61	46	25	18
Other[a]		.35–.46	.45–.51	22–68	21–62	25–59
Atlanta						
De Kalb	.35	.48	.64	55	21	2
Cobb	.40	.38	.55	12	71	36
Clayton	.26	.32	.56	89	44	−3
Other[a]		.19–.43	.22–.50	23–218	26–190	37–205
Cincinnati						
Boone	.32	.57	.66	53	7	−3
Other[a]		.23–.38	.29–.39	12–207	34–131	54–114
Columbus						
Union	.45	.43	.55	13	17	−22
Other[a]		.31–.42	.32–.42	4–55	17–70	24–78
Dallas						
All suburb counties[a]		.26–.43	.33–.37	40–112	37–171	60–161
Detroit						
Oakland	.37	.51	.62	35	20	10
Other[a]		.25–.40	.28–.45	16–118	24–159	17–138
Minneapolis						
Ramsey	.58	.68	.72	−21	−20	−22
Other[a]		.32–.42	.37–.44	44–107	49–95	70–84
Pittsburgh						
All suburb counties[a]		.28–.38	.27–.38	19–77	17–39	21–39
St. Louis						
St. Louis	.39	.55	.66	38	18	−4
Other[a]		.26–.42	.26–.44	6–152	9–182	20–166
Washington						
Arlington	.80	.96	1.28	−29	−39	−46
Montgomery	.43	.58	.67	44	23	14
Alexandria city[b]	.53	.79	1.05	23	−0.8	−16
Fairfax	.30	.45	.54	86	55	32
Other[a]		.18–.42	.22–.49	24–211	48–229	26–249

[a] Range.
[b] Independent City.

Note: E/Ps here are ratios of county employment (*place of work*) to county population. They differ from the E/Ps presented in Chapter 5, which are based on employment of residents. Resident adjustment percentages are calculated relative to total county earnings place of work.

Source: Data supplied by the Bureau of Economic Analysis.

Evidence of Suburban Agglomeration:
The County Data

The evidence that these agglomerations have increased i
in recent years raises a number of questions concerning
magnitude within the metropolitan system and the implica
growth and development for the continued viability of th
economy.

The analysis that follows seeks to assess the importanc€
economic agglomeration and to shed light on which among
and financial services have tended to locate within th€
centers.

Because only county data are available, much detail
suburban centers of the Hartshorn-Muller and the Cervero s
be pinpointed. Where they have developed within the centr
but outside the city itself no evidence can be garnered. Ye
to identify those suburban counties that have been most

Two types of evidence are examined. The first is the ratio c
to population. Here we look for high ratios indicating su
glomeration. We can also look for significant increases
especially since 1979, indicating those counties where the
large employment increases relative to any population ga

We also look at the residence adjustment expressed as
of total earnings of the county's work force. In evaluatir
this percentage over time, it is important to keep in n
residence adjustment is calculated by subtracting in-comm
from out-commuter earnings. A drop in the residence ad
centage indicates that *net* out-commuter earnings have de€
to all wages and salaries earned in the county workplace,
sign has switched from positive to negative, that net €
earnings have given way to net in-commuter earnings. Ir
in Table 4.3, the *value* of the residence adjustment (i.e., net €
earnings) could increase in dollar terms and yet decline as
of work force earnings (if the latter are increasing more

Among the counties that were selected as possible (can
"magnet" counties (Table 4.3), there is considerable var
measures. Yet in all there is a significant rise in the en
population ratio between 1979 and 1987 and in all but on€
County, a significant decline in the relative importance of €
earnings (although in most cases the residence adjustm
positive in 1987, indicating that, at least in terms of earni
all counties had some net out-migration, presumably to the

In certain counties, the residence adjustment measures have fallen precipitously. For example, in the Atlanta suburbs the residence adjustment percentage of workplace earnings for De Kalb was 55 in 1969, 21 in 1979, and 2 in 1987; in Cobb County, after rising from 12 percent in 1969 to 71 percent in 1979 (indicating increased commuting into Atlanta), it fell to 36 percent in 1987; and in Clayton County the measure fell from 89 percent in 1969 to 44 percent in 1979 and to -3 percent in 1987. In contrast, the residence adjustment percentage rose from 1969 to 1987 in most of the remaining counties in the Atlanta suburbs, and in all counties it stood at a higher level than in De Kalb, Cobb, or Clayton counties in the final year 1987. Moreover, whereas employment-to-population ratios in these three magnet counties stood at .64, .54, and .56, respectively, in 1987, in the remaining counties they ranged from .22 to .50.

It is interesting that a number of the counties shown in Table 4.3 are sites of suburban centers studied by Hartshorn and Muller or by Cervero. Montgomery and Camden counties in the Philadelphia suburbs and De Kalb and Cobb counties in the Atlanta suburbs are the locations of the King of Prussia, "Silicon Gulch," and Cherry Hill complexes and the Atlanta "suburban downtowns" described by Hartshorn and Muller. Seven of the counties are sites of suburban centers studied by Cervero: Middlesex (Boston): New England Executive Parks and Route 128 corridor; Ramsey (Minneapolis): 3M Parks; Nassau (New York): East Garden City and East Farmingdale; Du Page (Chicago): Naperville/I-88 Tollway; De Kalb (Atlanta): Perimeter Center and North Lake; Montgomery (Washington, D.C.): Rocksprings Park; Fairfax (Washington, D.C.): Tysons Corner.

Because the suburban counties shown in Table 4.3 stand out fairly clearly as areas of significant economic development, it is important to examine the relative size of these counties to assess the full significance of such development. Table 4.4 indicates the 1987 nonfarm employment in each of these counties alongside employment in the central city or central city county, with suburban county employment also shown as a percentage of central county employment.

The principal finding is that employment in most of these rapidly developing counties is relatively large. In St. Louis County, employment is more than twice that of the central city; in Middlesex County it is 47 percent larger. In Montgomery (Pennsylvania), Montgomery (Maryland), Norfolk (Massachusetts), De Kalb and Fairfax (Virginia), and De Kalb (Georgia), employment is more than half that of the central city, and in five of the remaining counties, more than one-fifth.

There are, however, two among the identified candidate counties that are quite small: Boone, in the suburbs of Cincinnati, and Union, in the

Table 4.4 Employment in Central City Counties and Candidate Magnet Counties, 1987

	Employment	Percentage of Central City County
New York (Manhattan)	2,679,977	100.0
Westchester	507,162	18.9
Nassau	784,494	29.3
Bergen	558,580	20.8
Chicago	1,330,029	100.0
Du Page	430,318	32.4
Philadelphia	869,654	100.0
Montgomery	492,299	56.6
Camden	245,482	28.2
Atlanta	685,290	100.0
De Kalb	346,638	50.6
Cobb	224,083	32.7
Clayton	94,144	13.7
Boston	656,311	100.0
Middlesex	962,718	146.7
Norfolk	373,374	56.9
Cincinnati	595,293	100.0
Boone	34,558	5.8
Columbus	625,175	100.0
Union	15,993	2.6
Detroit	1,021,050	100.0
Oakland	648,638	63.5
Minneapolis	856,530	100.0
Ramsey	341,464	39.9
St. Louis	330,240	100.0
St. Louis	662,852	200.7
Washington	740,671	100.0
Arlington	204,175	27.6
Montgomery	460,593	62.2
Alexandria	112,915	15.2
Fairfax	474,983	64.1

Note: Manhattan (New York County) is used here as the city county instead of the five boroughs combined. City of Chicago employment (estimated) is used here instead of Cook County employment. Chicago nonfarm business employment based on a special tabulation provided by BEA; government employment estimated by the author. All other "city" employment is central city county employment, BEA estimates.

Source: Data supplied by the Bureau of Economic Analysis.

Columbus suburbs. Moreover, there are two metropolitan areas, Dallas and Pittsburgh, in which no counties stood out. In the case of Dallas, rapid suburban economic development does not appear to have as yet extended to the suburban counties, although this is not to say that within the Dallas County suburbs no such development has occurred. We note that in all suburban counties in the Dallas metropolitan area, employment-to-population ratios are low (.37 or below) and the residence adjustment percentages quite high (60 to 161), indicating heavy commuting into Dallas County. In the case of Pittsburgh, we observe once again that employment-to-population ratios are low in all suburban counties, but residence adjustment percentages are also relatively low. Additional analysis is needed here, but the measures imply that the suburban counties in the Pittsburgh metropolitan area are characterized by relatively high unemployment and relatively low commutation and labor force participation rates.

Comparison of Central City and Magnet Suburban County Distributions of Employment and Levels of Earnings

Although the counties identified in Table 4.3 differ significantly in terms of industrial composition, they have to a great extent shared a common pattern of development. In virtually every county, the basic export sector in 1969 (manufacturing in all counties except the Washington, D.C., suburban counties, where government was the leading industrial category) declined sharply in importance, whereas other services and FIRE increased.[8] In roughly half of the counties, there was an increase in the relative importance of wholesaling and TCU, although in the remaining counties there was little change, with some decreases noted.

Table 4.5 compares central city and the candidate magnet suburban county shares of employment in manufacturing, TCU, wholesaling, retailing, FIRE, other services, and government. The principal observation is that although in manufacturing and retailing shares are larger in these suburban counties than in cities in a majority of 1987 comparisons, suburban county shares of employment in TCU, wholesaling, FIRE, and other services are substantial and in a number of instances larger than for the central city. In over half of the suburban counties, combined shares of other services and FIRE account for 40 percent or more of the county's total employment.

Three counties appear to be unlikely candidates for classification as magnet counties, however, and are not examined further. The first two are the very small counties of Union and Boone in the Columbus and Cincinnati metropolitan areas. Union is heavily specialized in manu-

Table 4.5 Shares (%) of City or Suburban County Employment by Industry, Central Cities, and Candidate Magnet Counties, 1987

	Manufacturing	TCU	Wholesale	Retail	FIRE	Other Services	Government
New York	9.6	5.9	6.3	11.0	14.7	34.5	14.4
Westchester	13.2*	4.8	6.3	15.4*	8.2	33.3	10.8
Nassau	10.8*	4.2	7.9*	17.4*	9.6	34.0	10.2
Bergen	18.0*	4.5	12.3*	16.1*	7.2	27.7	8.1
Chicago	17.4	6.7	5.7	13.2	12.4	29.4	11.8
Du Page	12.5	6.1	7.8*	18.2*	8.0	32.4*	8.0
Philadelphia	11.2	5.4	5.3	13.6	9.5	33.8	18.5
Montgomery	18.8*	3.3	5.7*	16.3*	10.1*	30.9	6.5
Camden	14.6*	4.3	7.7*	18.0*	7.6	28.4	13.1
Atlanta	8.6	9.4	9.7	13.8	10.4	29.6	13.8
De Kalb	9.5*	5.8	9.6	17.8*	10.1	28.4	11.7
Cobb	13.8*	4.1	9.5	18.9*	8.9	22.3	12.0
Clayton	6.7	21.1*	5.9	24.1*	4.1	14.6	15.5*
Boston	6.1	5.7	4.2	10.6	14.6	39.4	16.3
Middlesex	20.7*	3.1	6.2*	15.0*	5.5	34.3	9.5
Norfolk	13.7*	4.0	7.6*	17.9*	10.2	30.2	9.2
Cincinnati	20.3	4.9	6.7	16.3	8.0	28.3	10.4
Boone	20.1	13.3*	4.5	22.6*	4.0	21.3	8.5
Columbus	11.0	4.3	5.3	19.3	11.3	27.4	15.7
Union	48.4*	3.0	2.6	11.6	3.2	14.0	11.9
Detroit	22.7	5.8	5.3	15.9	6.8	26.8	13.4
Oakland	17.8	3.1	6.8*	21.5*	9.4*	35.7*	7.6
Minneapolis	15.0	5.7	7.7	16.4	10.3	29.2	11.0
Ramsey	23.4*	4.0	3.8	15.6*	7.8	27.1	13.9*
St. Louis	16.1	7.9	6.5	12.0	8.7	29.1	16.3
St. Louis	17.5*	5.2	6.1	18.2*	8.4	30.1*	8.0
Washington	2.3	3.6	1.2	7.9	6.4	36.8	39.0
Arlington	1.8	10.5*	3.5*	7.9	6.0	32.4	35.1
Montgomery	3.7*	2.4	3.9*	17.5*	9.5*	37.6*	17.2
Alexandria city	2.6*	5.7*	3.7*	16.5*	9.1*	33.9	11.5
Fairfax	4.1	4.5	4.3*	16.9*	10.3*	33.9	16.9

*In these cases, magnet county share exceeds central city share. Because primary industries are not shown, percentages do not add to 100.

Source: Data supplied by the Bureau of Economic Analysis.

facturing and Boone in retailing. The third is Clayton County, site of the Atlanta metropolitan airport, one of the busiest in the nation. In addition to airport facilities and airport-related activities, it is also a retailing center, but its other services sector is relatively underdeveloped.

A critical issue in examining the industrial composition of the remaining counties—those that appear to qualify as magnet counties—is the extent to which business and financial services have located there and whether, under conditions of relatively rapid employment growth in the suburbs, employment in these services threatens the economic vitality of the central city, where, traditionally, such economic activity has been centered.

Table 4.6 disaggregates employment within the large other-services category to reveal the relative size of the business-services segment along with that of three other categories, consumer services, social services, and repair services. The business-related services are further broken down into three standard industry classification (SIC) subgroups: SIC 73 (which includes a large variety of business services, principally advertising, credit reporting and collection, services to buildings, temporary-help agencies, computer and data processing services, and research and development); SIC 89 (principally engineering and architectural services and accounting auditing and bookkeeping); and SIC 81 (legal services).

We observe that business-related services play a substantial role in these counties. In Du Page, Montgomery (Pennsylvania), Camden, Middlesex, Oakland, and St. Louis counties, and in the four Washington suburban counties shown, the business-related services account for larger shares of total employment than in the central cities (Table 4.6). In most of the metropolitan areas, the FIRE share is largest in the central city, but this is not true for Montgomery (Maryland), Oakland, and three of the Washington suburban counties, where county shares are larger than in the central city (Table 4.5).

Within the business-related group (Table 4.6), the share of employment in legal services (SIC 81) are much larger in the central city than in the magnet counties in most metropolitan areas (two exceptions are Detroit and St. Louis). But this is not always true for either SIC 73 or SIC 89. Central city share is smaller than in one or more magnet suburban counties in a majority of comparisons for both of these subcategories.

It is interesting to examine shares in the business subcategories for the three largest metropolitan areas. Not surprisingly, central city shares are largest in all three categories in the New York comparison. But in the Chicago comparison, Du Page County has relatively larger employment (i.e., a larger share of employment) in SIC 73 than does the central city. In the comparison within the Philadelphia metropolitan

Table 4.6   Shares (%) of City or Suburban Employment in Other Services and Its Component Industry Groups, Central Cities and Magnet Counties, 1986

		Business-related						Total Other
	Consumer	SIC73	SIC89	SIC81	Total	Repair	Social	Services
New York (Manhattan)	4.0	11.2	2.8	2.7	16.7	0.5	11.6	33.2
Westchester	4.1*	7.2	1.5	0.7	9.3	1.3*	17.8*	32.7
Nassau	4.1*	9.3	2.5	1.2	13.1	1.3*	14.4*	33.4*
Bergen	3.8	8.3	2.2	0.7	11.2	1.5*	9.9	26.8
Chicago	3.4	8.6	2.4	2.3	13.2	1.1	15.0	33.3
Du Page	4.6*	13.0*	1.9	0.4	15.3*	1.9*	13.0	35.8*
Philadelphia	2.4	4.8	2.1	2.0	8.9	0.9	20.8	33.2
Montgomery	3.2*	8.4*	2.3*	0.4	11.1*	1.3*	14.2	30.1
Camden	3.3*	5.5	2.9*	1.3	9.7*	0.8	12.8	28.3
Atlanta	4.8	9.8	2.1	1.3	13.2	1.2	8.9	28.8
De Kalb	3.4	8.0	2.4*	0.5	10.9	1.2	10.9*	27.2
Cobb	4.9*	6.2	2.3*	0.5	9.0	1.1	6.8	22.0
Boston	3.2	7.3	3.5	2.4	13.2	1.0	21.4	39.1
Middlesex	2.2	10.0*	3.0	0.3	13.4*	0.9	15.4	33.6
Norfolk	3.0	7.3	2.6	0.5	10.4	1.3*	14.6	29.9
Detroit	2.8	5.0	1.2	0.8	7.0	1.5	14.6	26.0
Oakland	3.4*	11.0*	3.0*	1.1*	15.1*	1.2	12.1	32.2*
Minneapolis	4.0	8.2	1.9	1.1	11.2	1.1	11.8	28.8
Ramsey	2.7	5.6	1.4	0.8	7.8	1.0	14.7*	26.4
St. Louis	2.8	4.9	1.5	0.8	7.2	0.9	16.3	27.6
St. Louis	2.2	7.2*	2.2*	0.9*	10.2*	1.6*	15.1	29.9*
Washington	2.9	6.9	1.8	3.4	12.2	0.5	20.0	36.0
Arlington	4.6*	12.3*	4.9*	0.5	17.8*	1.1*	7.5	31.3
Montgomery	3.8*	15.3*	3.2*	0.7	19.3*	1.1*	11.9	37.3*
Alexandria	3.5*	10.4*	3.6*	0.9	14.9*	1.5*	11.8	32.6
Fairfax	3.7*	13.7*	5.7*	0.4	19.8*	0.9*	7.5	32.4

*In these cases, magnet county share exceeds central city share. Because primary industries are not shown, percentages do not add to 100.

Note: Cincinnati, Columbus, Dallas, and Pittsburgh are not shown because candidate magnet county was small or not identified. Percentages of component industries may not add to other services because administrative and auxiliary employment is not included. For definition of Chicago city see Note, Table 4.4. For definitions of SICs 73, 89, and 81, see text p. 71.

Source: Estimated from U.S. Bureau of the Census, County Business Patterns, 1986 (Washington, DC: GPO, 1987).

area, the suburban counties have relatively larger employment in both SIC 73 and 89 (although not in SIC 81).

In an effort to gain a clearer insight into the nature of central city versus suburban county comparative advantage, employment was examined in detailed FIRE and business-service subcategories for central city and selected suburban counties for New York, Chicago, Philadelphia, and Atlanta. In every county, employment in each industry subcategory was calculated as a percentage of the corresponding central city employment and adjusted to account for county size by dividing that percentage by the county's percentage of central city total employment. Thus, if Du Page County's employment in data processing was 47.67 percent of Chicago's employment in data processing, and its total employment was 34.40 percent of Chicago's total employment, the measure indicating importance of data processing in Du Page would be 1.39 (i.e., 47.67 ÷ 34.40).

Table 4.7 presents measures for a large number of detailed industry categories within SIC 73, SIC 89, and FIRE, as well as for legal services (SIC 81). To facilitate analysis, the indices described above were converted to three measures as follows: H (high)>120, M (medium)>80≤120, and L (low)<80.

An initial observation is that, except for credit agencies (SIC 61), the magnet counties in the New York and Chicago metros have relatively little employment in FIRE and legal services but are somewhat stronger in FIRE (although not in legal services) in the Philadelphia and Atlanta areas. In the various categories within the business-services group (SIC 73), however, the counties score M or H in a large majority of comparisons. Only in advertising (SIC 731), mailing, reproducing, and stenographic services (SIC 733), and services to buildings (SIC 734) do as many as three counties score L. In the two major categories of miscellaneous services (SIC 89), engineering, architectural services (SIC 891), and accounting auditing (SIC 893), no counties score H, but four out of five score M in SIC 891 and two out of five in SIC 893. Taken as a whole, the evidence indicates that these rapidly developing counties are establishing a strong economic base across a broad spectrum of business-related services.

Finally, comparison was made between average earnings in the seventeen magnet counties and their central cities for each of the major categories within other services and for FIRE (Table 4.8). County earnings were typically low relative to central city earnings for the consumer services group (average 72 percent of central city), legal services (average 83 percent), and FIRE (average 73 percent) but significantly higher for SIC 73 (average 102 percent), SIC 89 (average 88 percent), and social services (average 93 percent). In SIC 73, average earnings exceeded

Table 4.7 Scoring of Employment Levels in Detailed Industry Categories of FIRE, Business, Legal, and Miscellaneous Services, Five Magnet Counties, 1986

	New York		Chicago	Philadelphia	Atlanta	Tally		
	Nassau	Bergen	Du Page	Montgomery	De Kalb	L	M	H
6 FIRE								
60 Banking	L	L	L	M	M	3	2	0
61 Credit agencies	M	M	M	L	L	5	0	0
62 Security, commission brokers	L	L	L	H	H	0	3	2
63 Insurance carriers	M	L	L	H	M	5	0	0
64 Insurance agents, brokers	M	L	L	H	L	3	1	1
65 Real estate	H	L	L	L	M	4	0	1
67 Holding companies, other	M	L	L		L	5	1	1
Tally totals						25	6	4
7 Other Services (not inclusive)								
73 Business services	L	L	M	H	M			
731 Advertising[a]	H	L	L	M	L	1	3	1
732 Credit reporting, collection	M	M	L	H	H	4	1	0
733 Mailing, reproduction, stenographic	M	L	L	L	L	1	1	3
734 Services to buildings	M	L	L	H	L	4	1	0
736 Personnel supply	M	L	L	H	M	3	0	1
737 Computer, data processing services	H	H	M	H	M	0	3	2
739 Miscellaneous business services	M	H	H	H	NA	1	0	4
7391 R&D labs	M	L	L	H	M	0	2	2
7392 Management, public relations	H	H	H	M	M	1	3	4
7393 Detective, protective services	M	M	H	H	H	1	3	1
7394 Equipment rental	M	L	H	M	H	0	1	4
7395 Photo finishing	H	H	L	H	M	1	1	3
Tally totals						16	15	23
81 Legal services	L	L	L	L	L	5	0	0
89 Miscellaneous services	M	L	L	M	M	2	3	0
891 Engineering, architectural	M	M	L	M	M	1	4	0
893 Accounting, auditing	L	L	L	M	M	3	2	0
Tally totals						4	6	0

[a] Includes outdoor advertising and radio, TV representatives.

Notes: Scoring procedures for H (high), M (medium), and L (low) are described in text. Tally totals do not include categories: FIRE, SICs 73, 739, 81, 89.

Source: U.S. Bureau of the Census, *County Business Patterns, 1970, 1980, 1985* (Washington, DC: GPO, 1970, 1980, 1985).

Table 4.8 Average Earnings in Magnet Counties as a Percentage of Average Comparable Earnings in Central City County by Other Services Categories and FIRE, 1986

| | Consumer | Business-Related | | | Repair | Social | FIRE |
		SIC73	SIC89	SIC81			
New York (Manhattan)							
Westchester	55.4	69.5	82.6	77.3	93.7	82.6	43.5
Nassau	54.0	64.2	103.6	82.2	97.1	88.6	43.0
Bergen	57.8	75.5	102.3	61.6	98.5	88.6	46.5
Chicago							
Du Page	72.4	115.3	81.2	60.1	110.7	90.9	73.9
Philadelphia							
Montgomery	65.3	102.8	87.0	103.1	NA	86.4	76.7
Camden	69.9	123.2	104.7	98.1	NA	88.1	76.0
Atlanta							
De Kalb	83.2	101.7	100.1	78.8	93.8	96.4	71.0
Cobb	90.6	95.0	105.0	76.2	88.9	94.2	73.6
Boston							
Middlesex	74.0	122.8	85.6	66.0	133.7	89.8	62.9
Norfolk	100.4	96.9	79.1	64.2	120.2	95.7	56.2
Detroit							
Oakland	NA	131.9	111.8	111.3	103.2	107.6	95.2
Minneapolis							
Ramsey	74.5	79.8	102.6	87.6	98.5	93.3	86.6
St. Louis							
St. Louis	58.1	117.0	77.4	81.0	105.0	105.4	87.9
Washington							
Arlington	76.9	112.2	77.6	100.0	125.6	99.4	68.8
Montgomery	71.7	108.5	68.3	91.7	136.0	89.0	86.6
Alexandria	78.3	102.7	63.3	82.4	119.7	104.0	87.1
Fairfax	78.7	115.0	66.8	100.6	152.3	76.1	91.1
Modified average[a]	71.9	102.5	88.3	83.4	110.0	92.8	72.6

[a] In computing modified averages, lowest and highest values are dropped.

Note: For definitions of SICs 73, 89, and 81, see text, p. 71.

Source: Data supplied by the Bureau of Economic Analysis.

central city levels in eleven of the counties; in SIC 89, in seven. In consumer services, legal services, social services, and FIRE, the number of counties in which average earnings exceeded central city levels was quite small: one, four, three, and zero, respectively.

Closer examination of the measures indicates considerable variation in business-service earnings levels among counties within and among metropolitan areas, suggesting different patterns of city-suburban specialization within and among the various metropolitan areas. For example, in the three New York suburban counties, average earnings in SIC 73 were well below Manhattan levels, although in two counties SIC 89 earnings were above; in Du Page, the opposite was the case.

In general, the earnings evidence complements the evidence gleaned from the employment data. Central cities demonstrate a strong comparative advantage in most FIRE activities and in legal services: Employment in these activities is relatively larger and earnings higher. It is here that the special agglomeration economies of the central business district are most pronounced, although a few types of FIRE activities, such as credit agencies and insurance carriers, may operate successfully as a part of the export base of the suburban economy. Moreover, the relatively low earnings levels in FIRE in the suburban counties indicate the predominance of routine consumer banking and real estate services and suggest the presence of back-office activities, whereas lower earnings levels in legal services indicate that law firms are relatively unspecialized with relatively few highly paid personnel.

Among the business services, these well-developed suburban counties are often quite successful in attracting firms that pay, on average, wages and salaries much closer to central city levels than is true for most other industrial classifications. In some activities, such as data processing and research and development, firms find highly favorable conditions for locating. Professional-type business-related services also often do well in these counties, although the data (not shown in Table 4.8) suggest that engineering and architectural firms are more frequently found in the suburbs than are accounting and auditing firms.

The relatively low suburban earnings levels in consumer services shown in Table 4.8 reflect to a considerable extent a difference in mix between central city and county, the central city typically showing relatively more employment in hotels and amusements; the suburbs, relatively more employment in personal services. An additional factor is the greater tendency to utilize part-time personnel in the suburbs (see Chapter 5).

Earnings in the social-services are for the most part higher in the central city, but the differences are typically not great. It is interesting that the city-suburban differentials shown for social services in Table 4.8 are, almost without exception, roughly the same as for health services (not shown), the largest category within the social-services group. Apparently, the differentials noted for earnings in the social services reflect some combination of (1) the degree of specialization in the services (e.g., central city hospitals are likely to be larger—although there are also large complexes in many of the leading suburban counties) and (2) differences in central city and suburban wage levels.

Central City and Suburbs:
Competition or Symbiosis?

In Chapter 2 it was shown that both central city and suburb have experienced dramatic transformations since the 1960s and that these transformations have brought about a major restructuring to accommodate the business environment to the new economic era in which services—especially business and financial services—play a key role in economic development. In both central city and suburb, this restructuring has brought about a new set of locational attractions.

The principal finding thus far in this chapter is that in the suburbs development appears to have been increasingly focussed on a limited number of centers with large shares of employment provided by in-commuters (although in most of the counties in which these centers are located there continues to be a *net* outflow of commuters because of the continued dominant role of the central city and its increased need for a skilled, educated work force).

A second major finding is that in a variety of business-related services the key counties have succeeded in attracting large numbers of workers, although in some, the central cities have retained a distinct advantage. Moreover, magnet county earnings levels in a number of activities indicate a relatively heavy employment of well-paid workers.

These findings give rise to new questions regarding the future relationship of central city and suburb. With employment growth in the suburbs continuing to outpace that in the city and with suburban agglomerations developing and becoming increasingly attractive as business locations, is there a new threat to the city's vitality? To what extent do the economies of central cities and their suburbs complement each other and to what extent do they compete?

In a recent study of the greater metropolitan New York City economy, Matthew Drennan observed that the central city's economy has developed by a process of taking on more highly value-added functions, whereas the suburbs have developed through a process involving "a passing down of functions"—a sorting out of those activities that can be successfully and more cheaply carried out away from the congested and high-cost environment of the city.[9] His conclusion is that although suburban growth has been relatively rapid, it has not been at the expense of the New York City economy. The relationship is essentially symbiotic, not competitive. Economies of agglomeration in the central city allow it to successfully hold on to—and spawn—a variety of high value-added activities while other activities appropriately locate in the suburbs.

But as one examines the data it becomes difficult to argue that this continuous renewal of the central city's economy need always take place—or that, if it does, it will proceed at a sufficiently rapid pace so that the export base and, in turn, the central city's economy itself will not be eroded. The New York story may be different from the others: There may be other models applicable to other metropolitan areas. New York, with its strong central city and dominant role as the United States' principal world city, contrasts with, say, Philadelphia, which appears to be losing certain functions to its suburbs. The heavy losses in Philadelphia and Boston during the 1970s and in St. Louis during both the 1970s and 1980s, at a time when the suburbs continued to grow and develop, would hardly indicate that these central cities did not suffer, at least to some extent, from competition in their suburbs.

Of course, there is considerable evidence that the major cities have gone far to revitalize their economies. Frieden's apt description of the physical and cultural rebuilding of America's major cities attests to this renewal. The earnings and employment data analyzed earlier provide evidence that central city economies have become more narrowly focussed and have upgraded their specializations.

Yet there is also evidence that the suburban economies are changing and growing in strength. Although it is clear that the cities retain their advantage in high-level FIRE and legal services, it is also apparent that the key suburban counties have gained in their ability to attract a variety of business services, as well as wholesaling and social services.

This is not to argue that the large central city does not continue to be the favored location for a variety of specialized activities that are best served by its special business and cultural environment. But the growth and maturation of the suburbs—especially insofar as the suburban developmental process has been strengthened by the development of magnet centers—must, of necessity, alter the relationship between central city and suburbs. In this new relationship, it would appear that central cities may become more vulnerable to competition, at least in those activities for which their comparative advantage is marginal.

Competition from Outside the Metropolis

It is important to recognize also that competition and metropolitan development are taking place within a nationwide system of metropolitan economies. New York City competes not only with its suburbs for a new corporate headquarters or regional sales office; it and its suburbs also compete with a number of other cities and their suburbs, including not only very large places such as Chicago, San Francisco, and Los Angeles but also smaller but nevertheless highly developed urban centers such as Atlanta, Dallas, and Phoenix.

Table 4.9 Change in Location of Fortune 500 Industrial and Service Corporation Headquarters, 1970–1979, 1979–1983, 1983–1988

	Industrial			Service	
	1970	*1979*	*1988*	*1983*	*1988*
New York (Manhattan)	117	78	50	56	66
Chicago	39	24	21	18	20
Los Angeles	13	12	10	19	18
Philadelphia	10	7	6	9	9
	179	122	87	102	113
Change		−57	−35	+11	
New York Suburbs	34	54	50	23	17
Chicago Suburbs	15	21	20	12	11
Los Angeles Suburbs	10	12	8	26	21
Philadelphia Suburbs	4	5	3	3	5
	63	92	81	64	54
Change		+29	−11	−10	
Dallas	7	8	16	19	20
Atlanta	3	4	10	7	10
Minneapolis–St. Paul	11	11	16	11	14
Washington	0	3	7	7	9
	21	26	49	44	53
Change		+5	+23	+9	

Source: Thierry Noyelle, unpublished data.

In the new U.S. economy, corporations are changing their locational strategies to take account of the need to be more closely related to regional needs and to respond to the changing locational attractions that arise out of the increasing importance of environmental considerations or proximity to major universities and research and development facilities. In a recent study, Thierry Noyelle compared the number of Fortune 500 headquarters located in the cities and suburbs of New York, Chicago, Philadelphia, and Los Angeles and in four smaller cities, Dallas, Atlanta, Minneapolis–St. Paul, and Atlanta, in different years: for Fortune 500 industrial firms, 1970, 1979, and 1988 and for Fortune 500 service firms, 1983 and 1988 (Table 4.9). During the 1970s, the large cities lost fifty-seven industrial headquarters, a 32 percent decrease, while their suburbs gained twenty-nine, a 46 percent increase; the smaller cities gained five headquarters, a 24 percent increase. During the 1980s, the large cities lost thirty-five headquarters, a decrease of 29 percent; their suburbs lost eleven, a 12 percent decrease; the smaller cities, however, posted a whopping gain of twenty-three headquarters, an 88 percent increase. During the 1983–1988 period, the large cities gained eleven Fortune 500 service corporations, an 11 percent increase; their suburbs lost ten, a

Table 4.10   Administrative and Auxiliary Employment, 1970, 1980, 1985

		Administrative and Auxiliary Employment (in thousands)			Annual Rate of Change	
		1970	1980	1985	1970–80	1980–85
Cities						
New York	Total	198.5	164.0	150.8	−1.9	−1.7
	Manufacturing	122.6	78.1	59.8	−4.3	−5.2
	Other	75.9	85.9	91.0	1.3	1.1
Chicago	Total	128.1	130.9	121.8	0.2	−1.5
	Manufacturing	65.3	65.8	53.9	0.1	−3.9
	Other	62.8	65.1	67.9	0.4	0.8
Philadelphia	Total	33.3	25.0	35.2	−2.8	7.1
	Manufacturing	13.6	7.5	7.8	−5.7	0.8
	Other	19.7	17.5	27.4	−1.2	9.4
Suburbs						
New York	Total	30.6	69.3	67.1	8.5	−0.7
	Manufacturing	23.2	41.0	33.0	5.8	−4.2
	Other	7.4	28.3	34.1	14.3	3.8
Chicago	Total	10.6	37.2	50.7	13.4	6.4
	Manufacturing	6.5	24.2	25.5	14.0	0.8
	Other	4.1	13.0	25.2	12.2	14.1
Philadelphia	Total	19.8	55.5	64.6	10.9	3.1
	Manufacturing	15.2	33.8	34.6	8.3	0.5
	Other	4.6	21.7	30.0	16.8	6.6

Source: U.S. Bureau of the Census, *County Business Patterns, 1970, 1980, 1985* (Washington, DC: GPO, 1970, 1980, 1985).

16 percent decrease; the smaller cities showed a gain of nine, clearly the largest relative gain, 20 percent.

These findings are to a considerable degree supported by *County Business Patterns* estimates for administrative and auxiliary employment (A&A, or employment in freestanding administrative units, including headquarters, sales, etc.) in the New York City, Philadelphia, and Chicago metropolitan areas. These data (Table 4.10) show that suburbs gained sharply in A&A employment during the 1970s, much less rapidly in the 1980s (there were declines in the New York suburbs). The three central cities lost administrative and auxiliary employment or made only a small gain during the 1970s. During the 1980s, New York and Chicago continued to lose, although Philadelphia made a sharp gain. When the administrative and auxiliary data are broken down between manufacturing and all other industries (almost entirely services), we observe that manufacturing tended to fare much worse than service activities during both periods in both cities and suburbs. Presumably, the administrative activities of manufacturing have moved more readily to other locales than have other activities, although experience has differed somewhat between cities and suburbs and among places.

Conclusion

The principal finding of this chapter is that suburban economic development does not take place evenly across the outlying metropolitan area but rather is centered in key or magnet areas where economies of agglomeration arise, growth is rapid, and the export sector develops. In the remaining counties of the suburbs, economic activities are more heavily focussed on providing services to residents, and a larger share of income is derived from the earnings of commuters—to the central city and to the growing magnet centers of the suburbs.

Not only do these developing economic centers of the suburbs bring new competition to the central city, but there is also increasing competition from other metropolitan economies. Accordingly, it becomes of primary importance to identify and examine those problems that threaten the competitive strength of these economies and to direct public policy toward their solution. If policy considerations also involve addressing major social issues, then economic necessity adds a new dimension to the need for action.

For most large central cities, the foremost problem is that there is a large segment of the population that has not been drawn into its productive work force but lies on the periphery of the labor market, dependent on municipal services and constituting a drain upon the cities' resources.

The next chapter examines the population and work force characteristics of cities and suburbs of the four largest metropolitan areas in this study. The final chapter assesses problems of both central city and suburb and suggests priorities in framing public policy.

Notes

1. This and the preceding three paragraphs are taken virtually verbatim from a study prepared by the staff of the Conservation of Human Resources project at Columbia University, *The Corporate Headquarters Complex in New York City* (New York, NY: Conservation of Human Resources, Columbia University, 1977).

2. Bernard J. Frieden, "The Downtown Job Puzzle," *The Public Interest* 97(Fall 1989):73.

3. Frieden, "The Downtown Job Puzzle," pp. 71–73.

4. Truman A. Hartshorn and Peter O. Muller, *Suburban Business Centers: Employment Expectations*, Final Report for U.S. Department of Commerce, EDA (Washington, DC: Department of Commerce, November 1986), p. 3.

5. Hartshorn and Muller, *Suburban Business Centers*, p. 1.

6. For a complete description of stages, see Hartshorn and Muller, *Suburban Business Centers*, pp. 19–31.

7. Truman A. Hartshorn and Peter O. Muller, "Suburban Downtowns and the Transformation of Metropolitan Atlanta's Business Landscape," *Urban Geography* 10(4):384.

8. This was not the case in Union County (Columbus metropolitan area), where manufacturing employment grew sharply throughout both periods.

9. Matthew Drennan, "The Local Economy," in Charles Brecher and Raymond D. Horton, eds., *Setting Municipal Priorities, 1990* (New York, NY: New York University Press, 1989), pp. 27ff.

5

Population and Work Force Characteristics

The preceding chapters set forth many of the essential differences between city and suburban economies. They do not, however, tell us how successful various groups have been in finding jobs, nor do they indicate those industries in which such groups have tended to find employment most readily. In this chapter following a brief discussion of data sources, we look first at certain major differences between city and suburban populations and then examine evidence, based largely on employment-to-population ratios, of how well or how poorly the several groups of workers fared in finding employment. The following section inquires further into the employment experience and educational qualifications of resident workers by examining data at the industry level for various groups of workers. A final section evaluates the significance of the analyses. The analysis throughout is limited to the four largest metropolitan areas—New York, Chicago, Philadelphia, and Los Angeles.

The Current Population Survey Material

Much of the analysis in this chapter is based on special tabulations from the *Current Population Survey* (CPS) data base. This data base offers the investigator a unique opportunity to examine changing employment patterns in large metropolitan areas. Information is drawn annually from a population sample constructed for year-to-year comparability. The advantages of the CPS data over other data sources available on an annual basis are chiefly: (1) A wide variety of information is obtained from each individual sampled (e.g., employment status, sex, age, race, level of educational attainment, industry of employment, hours worked); (2) respondent's place of residence (city or suburb) is defined by municipal rather than the central city county boundaries, and suburbs are defined as the remainder of the metropolitan area; and (3) information is obtained for the entire population sampled, both those who are employed and those who are not.

The chief disadvantage is that sample sizes are relatively small and that reliability declines significantly as smaller subsets of the data are examined. In this analysis, a number of commonsense concessions have been made to the problem of sample size by avoiding certain subdivisions of the data (e.g., industry breakdowns are not subdivided by both race and age). In general, the reader must keep in mind that findings relating to smaller subsets (e.g., industry-sex-age) are less reliable than findings relating to larger subsets.

In addition, it is important to point out that the CPS data relate to place of residence of the worker, not to his or her place of work. For some analyses, such as preparation of employment-to-population ratios, place-of-residence data are appropriate. But for other analyses, such as the industrial composition of the work force, place-of-work data should be used.

Because only place-of-residence data are available in the CPS data base, it is important to understand the difference in the two types of data sets and to assess the extent to which use of place-of-residence rather than place-of-work data may affect the analysis. What must be kept in mind is that place-of-residence data do not include a sizable number of in-commuters from the suburbs who are likely to be white, work full time, and have an average or better education. These commuters also are likely to be disproportionately male. Similarly, we must recognize that the suburban resident worker data include these same commuters, although they work elsewhere.

Finally, it should be pointed out that the industrial classifications are those used previously, except that the other-services group is omitted. Three subcategories of other services are presented: business/repair (the business-related and repair service categories used earlier are combined), consumer, and social. The latter two are the same as those presented in previous chapters.

Population and Work Force Characteristics

Observations Based on Population Data

Three observations may be made on the basis of the population data, which, though not unexpected, serve to establish fundamental differences between the labor forces of central city and suburban economies.

Size of Minority Population. The first is simply that minority populations are larger in the central cities (Table 5.1). In 1985, ethnic minorities accounted for from 25 to 44 percent of the working-age (16

Table 5.1   Percentage Distribution of Population Aged 16–65 Among Races and Percentage of Population Aged 16–19, 1980, 1985

	New York		Chicago		Philadelphia		Los Angeles	
	1980	*1985*	*1980*	*1985*	*1980*	*1985*	*1980*	*1985*
Distribution (%)								
Aged 16–65								
City								
White	67.9	68.8	59.2	55.5	62.6	56.2	76.7	74.9
Black	27.1	26.6	38.1	40.1	35.7	42.5	16.0	14.7
Other	5.0	4.6	2.7	4.3	1.7	1.3	7.3	10.4
Total	100.0	100.0	100.0	100.0	100.0	100.0	100.0	100.0
Suburbs								
White	91.4	89.8	93.8	91.0	91.1	93.0	81.6	84.7
Black	8.0	7.4	5.0	8.1	8.2	6.7	9.5	6.1
Other	0.6	2.8	1.2	0.8	0.7	0.3	8.9	9.1
Total	100.0	100.0	100.0	100.0	100.0	100.0	100.0	100.0
Aged 16–19 as percentage of								
City								
Whites	9.1	8.3	10.7	7.5	10.1	8.9	9.1	8.7
All minorities	14.6	12.5	15.2	12.6	14.9	10.6	8.1	11.6
Suburbs								
Whites	11.1	9.6	11.6	8.3	11.1	9.9	12.2	8.4
All minorities	11.3	13.1	11.8	7.4	17.3	19.4	14.9	7.7

Source: Compiled from *Current Population Survey* data supplied by the Bureau of the Census.

to 65 years) city populations, from 7 to 15 percent of the comparable suburban populations. In New York, Chicago, and Philadelphia, the difference in relative size of city and suburban minority population was quite large (21 to 35 percentage points); in Los Angeles it was much smaller (10 percentage points). In Chapter 1, we saw that in Los Angeles commuter flows into and out of the city were much more evenly matched than in the other larger metropolitan areas. Here is evidence once again that in the Los Angeles metropolitan area city and suburbs are less clearly differentiated.

Minorities, 16–19 Years of Age. The second finding is that in all four of the central cities, the 16–19-year-old minority cohort accounts for a much larger share of the entire minority population (16–65 years) than does the 16–19-year-old white cohort of the total white population (Table 5.1). This means that in the cities the share of 16–19-year-olds accounted for by minorities is larger than the minority's share of the entire working-age population (Table 5.2). Table 5.2 shows that in the suburbs of New York and Philadelphia the share of 16–19-year-olds accounted for by minorities is also larger than is the minority's share of the entire working-

Table 5.2   Percentage Minority Share of City and Suburban Population, 1985

	New York	Chicago	Philadelphia	Los Angeles
Cities				
Minority share of:				
16–19-year-old cohort	40.5	57.2	48.1	30.8
Total working-age population	31.2	38.2	41.6	25.1
Suburbs				
Minority share of:				
16–19-year-old cohort	13.4	7.1	12.8	14.2
Total working-age population	10.2	7.6	7.0	15.2

Source: Compiled from *Current Population Survey* data supplied by the Bureau of the Census.

Table 5.3   Percentage Distribution of Population Aged 16–65 by Educational Attainment, 1980, 1985

	New York		Chicago		Philadelphia		Los Angeles	
	1980	*1985*	*1980*	*1985*	*1980*	*1985*	*1980*	*1985*
Cities								
< HS	36.2	32.8	41.9	35.0	40.3	32.0	27.6	30.1
≥ HS < 2 yrs college	40.2	38.9	36.7	36.8	44.0	49.7	37.2	34.5
≥ 2 yrs college	23.6	28.3	21.4	28.3	15.7	18.3	35.2	35.4
Suburbs								
< HS	20.6	13.9	18.9	15.5	24.0	18.7	26.9	27.7
≥ HS < 2 yrs college	47.1	47.3	46.7	45.4	46.5	52.8	41.5	38.7
≥ 2 yrs college	32.3	38.8	34.3	39.1	29.5	28.5	31.6	33.6

Source: Compiled from *Current Population Survey* data supplied by the Bureau of the Census.

age population. Nevertheless, suburban shares are far below those for these central cities.

The above estimates serve to make clear that minorities account for a very large share of the cities' young people who are eligible to enter the job market, much larger than in the suburbs. Because it is the minority population that is most disadvantaged in finding work, city labor markets clearly face much greater problems in providing the kinds of jobs suitable for the least skilled than do the suburbs.

Levels of Educational Attainment. The third observation is that in all four metropolitan areas, levels of education were higher in the suburbs than in the central cities (Table 5.3).

Patterns of change in educational attainment levels between 1980 and 1985 have varied among metropolitan areas. In New York and Chicago, city and suburban shares of the population with less than a high school diploma declined and shares of college graduates increased. This was true also for Philadelphia city, although in the suburbs the share of college graduates declined slightly, whereas a larger percentage had a high school diploma but less than two years of college. In Los Angeles city and suburbs, on the other hand, there were small increases in the percentage of the population with less than a high school education. Only in the suburbs was there significant improvement of any kind— a 2 percent increase in the share of those with two or more years of college.

Employment: A Look at the Employment/Population Ratios

Men and Women. Comparison of employment/population (E/P) ratios indicates that in New York, Chicago, and Philadelphia residents fared better in gaining employment (ratios were higher) in suburbs than in cities (Table 5.4).[1] This finding holds for both males and females in every comparison, although of course E/P ratios were higher for males than for females. The principal explanation of this city-suburban difference would appear to be that these cities have much larger groups of the hard-to-employ—minorities and others—whereas suburbs have a smaller share of such groups and at the same time a better-educated and more employable labor force. But the difference comes about at least in part because larger numbers of suburban workers than city workers find work as commuters, adding to the E/P ratios of the suburbs and tending to reduce the E/P ratios of the city. At the same time, the larger residentiary sector in the suburbs, along with back-office activity and a larger manufacturing base, offers a wider range of job opportunities for suburban women and young workers.

The experience within the Los Angeles metropolitan area is somewhat different. There is virtually no difference in ratios in city and suburbs. Here we observe still further evidence that city and suburbs are less differentiated in Los Angeles than elsewhere.

The Young. In New York, Chicago, and Philadelphia, young people, both male and female, fared much worse in employment terms in cities than in suburbs: E/P ratios for 16–19-year-olds were sharply lower in the cities than in suburbs (Table 5.4). The city-suburb differences in E/P ratios for these metropolitan areas are far greater for the young than for all age groups combined. Clearly, the young of these cities, with their lower levels of educational achievement and large shares of disadvantaged minorities, face formidable obstacles in finding work. Moreover, as will be discussed below, these city economies offer relatively few jobs suitable for the inexperienced and poorly educated than do the suburbs.

Table 5.4 Selected Employment/Population Ratios (E/Ps), 1985 and E/P 1985 / E/P 1980

	E/P 1985				E/P 1985 / E/P 1980			
	New York	Chicago	Philadelphia	Los Angeles	New York	Chicago	Philadelphia	Los Angeles
All races								
City								
Male	0.67	0.66	0.69	0.76	0.91	0.96	1.11	0.94
Female	0.50	0.54	0.46	0.57	1.04	1.04	0.92	0.95
Total	0.57	0.58	0.56	0.66	0.99	0.98	1.01	0.95
Suburbs								
Male	0.81	0.85	0.82	0.78	1.00	1.00	0.99	0.99
Female	0.59	0.66	0.60	0.57	1.15	1.10	1.07	0.94
Total	0.68	0.74	0.71	0.67	1.06	1.05	1.03	0.97
Aged 16–19 years								
City								
Male	0.12	0.30	0.12	0.36	0.64	0.84	0.56	0.68
Female	0.16	0.24	0.27	0.29	0.94	1.40	0.79	0.71
Suburbs								
Male	0.38	0.52	0.56	0.31	1.03	1.01	1.12	0.63
Female	0.37	0.53	0.56	0.27	1.11	0.94	1.12	0.67
Race								
City								
Male								
White	0.71	0.76	0.77	0.82	0.90	0.95	1.06	0.96
Black	0.55	0.55	0.67	0.66	0.92	1.14	1.47	0.92
Other				0.66				0.84
Female								
White	0.51	0.58	0.56	0.62	1.01	1.01	1.00	1.02
Black	0.48	0.48	0.38	0.48	1.16	1.12	0.87	0.79
Other				0.47				0.74

	E/P 1985				E/P 1985 / E/P 1980			
	New York	Chicago	Philadelphia	Los Angeles	New York	Chicago	Philadelphia	Los Angeles
Race (continued)								
Suburbs								
Male								
White	0.82	0.87	0.87	0.81	1.01	1.02	1.00	0.97
Black	0.69	0.66	0.54	0.63	1.00	0.80	0.86	0.91
Other				0.88				1.20
Female								
White	0.59	0.66	0.62	0.58	1.17	1.11	1.10	0.94
Black	0.62	0.77	0.55	0.50	1.04	0.99	1.02	0.84
Other				0.62				1.04
Educational attainment								
City								
Male								
< HS	0.46	0.51	0.36	0.67	0.81	0.95	0.81	0.90
≥ HS < 2 yrs college	0.71	0.73	0.82	0.75	0.94	0.91	1.15	0.94
≥ 2 yrs college	0.85	0.77	0.91	0.89	0.92	0.97	1.07	0.97
Female								
< HS	0.27	0.33	0.27	0.39	0.96	0.93	0.87	0.99
≥ HS < 2 yrs college	0.52	0.58	0.49	0.62	0.96	1.02	0.85	1.00
≥ 2 yrs college	0.75	0.75	0.77	0.72	1.05	0.97	1.03	0.94
Suburbs								
Male								
< HS	0.59	0.78	0.65	0.61	1.06	1.01	1.00	0.87
≥ HS < 2 yrs college	0.80	0.84	0.90	0.83	0.95	1.00	1.06	1.02
≥ 2 yrs college	0.90	0.89	0.82	0.92	0.99	0.99	0.87	1.04
Female								
< HS	0.34	0.59	0.38	0.33	1.10	1.14	1.01	0.77
≥ HS < 2 yrs college	0.58	0.65	0.61	0.62	1.08	1.08	0.98	0.99
≥ 2 yrs college	0.70	0.72	0.71	0.76	1.11	1.08	1.20	0.95

Note: E/Ps based on employed residents.

Source: Compiled from Current Population Survey data supplied by the Bureau of the Census.

When E/P ratios of young men and young women are compared within these cities, young men are found to have fared worse in New York and Philadelphia but somewhat better in Chicago. In the suburbs, however, E/P ratios were virtually the same for young men and women in each comparison.

Finally, when 1985 E/P ratios of these three metropolitan areas are compared with those for 1980, young males in the cities are found to have been employed in relatively fewer numbers at middecade than at the beginning. E/P ratios for young women also declined in two of these cities (New York and Philadelphia), but to a lesser degree. In the suburbs, however, E/P ratios increased or remained unchanged in virtually all comparisons.

The E/P data tell a somewhat different story for the Los Angeles area: Here E/P ratios for young men were about the same in city as in suburbs in 1985. This was true of young women as well, although their E/P levels were somewhat lower. However, 1985 E/P levels in city and suburbs were much lower than 1980, with declines roughly the same for males and females.

Blacks. The principal finding from the E/P ratios for blacks is that, with the exception of black women in the New York and Chicago suburbs, blacks fared worse than whites in both cities and suburbs of all four metropolitan areas in 1985 (Table 5.4).

Improvement in the employment of blacks in terms of increases in E/Ps (1980–1985) was limited, with significant gains noted only in Chicago and Philadelphia cities for males and New York and Chicago cities for females. In other comparisons, E/Ps declined or remained virtually unchanged.

Because of the small size of "other minorities" in New York, Chicago, and Philadelphia cities and suburbs, E/P data are not shown for these groups. The E/P ratios for other minorities are shown for Los Angeles, however, and indicate a better work experience in the suburbs than in the city: In the city E/P levels for males and females were low, roughly the same as for blacks; in the suburbs they were somewhat higher than for blacks. In the city these E/P ratios had declined from 1980 levels; in the suburbs they had risen.

Workers Grouped by Levels of Education. When 1985 E/P ratios for the three educational attainment groups are compared for males and females in cities and suburbs, we find clear evidence of the increased employability that goes with more schooling (Table 5.4). In every city and suburb, E/P ratios are lower for workers with less than a high school education than for workers with more, and only among males in the suburbs of Philadelphia are ratios for workers with two or more

Table 5.5   Percentage of Resident Workers with Less Than a High School Education, 1985

	New York		Chicago		Philadelphia		Los Angeles	
	City	*Suburb*	*City*	*Suburb*	*City*	*Suburb*	*City*	*Suburb*
Males	22.6	10.3	28.5	14.5	19.9	18.1	24.7	21.0
Females	17.5	7.7	20.1	13.6	19.8	11.6	21.1	15.9

Source: Compiled from *Current Population Survey* data supplied by the Bureau of the Census.

years of college below those for workers with a high school degree but less than two years of college.

The employment experience of those without a high school diploma merits special comment. Although E/P ratios for the poorly educated are much lower for cities than for suburbs, these workers account for a larger *share* of the resident work force in each city (Table 5.5).

What we are observing here is that the cities' labor markets have in fact made considerable accommodation to the very large labor supply of poorly educated persons—yet not enough to bring E/P ratios to suburban levels. The net result is high unemployment in the cities among certain minority groups who are characterized by disproportionately larger numbers of the poorly educated.

Unfortunately, there is evidence that the situation of poorly educated city workers grows worse (Table 5.4): During the 1980–1985 period, E/P ratios for those with the least education declined in all four cities yet remained at 1980 levels or improved in the suburbs except in Los Angeles.

Employment Experience: A Closer Look

The preceding section has treated the questions of how well or how poorly several groups—women, the young, minorities—have fared in gaining employment in cities and suburbs and the extent to which education is linked to success in finding jobs. In the present section, attention shifts to analysis of the distribution among industries of each group of workers and to examination of part-time employment. Such analysis is useful on two counts. First, it tells us something about the industries themselves, whether hiring organizations tend to make heavy or light use of part-time workers, women, minorities, or the poorly educated. Second, it provides, by inference, an indication of where individuals in those groups with the lowest E/P ratios who do gain employment are most likely—and least likely—to find jobs.

Industrial Distribution
of Male and Female Employment

Although their relatively rapid increase in employment over several decades has brought women a wider variety of job opportunities, the industrial distribution of employment of female resident workers in the four metropolitan areas remained significantly different from that of males in 1985, both in central cities and in suburbs. This is readily seen in Tables 5.6 and 5.7, which show the distribution of male and female employment in cities and suburbs along with concentration ratios (C/Rs). These ratios facilitate analysis by indicating how the share of male or female employment in a given industry compares to the share of total employment accounted for by combined male and female employment in the same industry.[2]

In both cities and suburbs, employment of women tends to be relatively concentrated in FIRE, consumer services, and social services; employment of men, in construction, manufacturing, TCU, wholesaling, and government. The large retailing sector provides substantial employment for workers of both sexes, with female employment tending to be relatively more important in suburbs, male employment relatively more important in cities. In general, women's jobs tend to be most heavily concentrated in social services—26 to 41 percent of all their employment in cities, 28 to 35 percent in suburbs. Men tend to be most heavily concentrated in manufacturing—19 to 28 percent of their employment in cities (excluding New York), 19 to 30 percent in suburbs. Across the spectrum of industry classifications, women's jobs tend to be more heavily concentrated in a few industries than men's.

Black Men and Women

In looking to industry data to shed additional light on the employment experience of black men and women, we examine once again the distribution of employment, i.e., the shares of employment of black men or black women accounted for by each industry. Analysis is limited to cities because the small numbers of blacks employed in the suburbs make CPS sampling unreliable. Once again, analysis focuses on whether the share of black male (female) employment accounted for by a given industry is larger or smaller than the comparable share for whites. Table 5.8 presents tallies for each industry indicating the number of cities in which shares of black males (females) are greater (smaller) than comparable shares for whites.

The principal finding is that black men appear to have more limited access across industry lines than do white men. Employed black men tend to find relatively fewer jobs (i.e., shares are smaller than whites'

Table 5.6 Percentage Distribution and Concentration Ratios (C/Rs) of Male Employed Residents by Industry, 1985

	New York		Chicago		Philadelphia		Los Angeles		Tally: C/Rs		
	Distribution	C/R	Distribution	C/R	Distribution	C/R	Distribution	C/R	>1.0	1.0	<1.0
City											
Construction	5.4	1.6	5.1	1.7	6.4	1.9	5.5	1.5	4	—	—
Manufacturing	13.1	0.9	28.2	1.3	18.5	1.1	25.8	1.2	3	—	1
TCU	14.8	1.4	12.1	1.1	11.6	1.5	5.5	1.0	3	1	—
Wholesale	4.0	1.3	4.0	1.1	3.3	1.1	3.1	1.0	3	1	—
Retail	13.0	1.2	16.1	1.0	14.5	1.1	18.1	1.1	3	1	—
FIRE	13.5	1.0	4.8	0.6	4.3	0.8	7.3	0.8	—	1	3
Business/repair services	7.7	1.0	7.3	0.9	9.7	1.1	9.8	1.2	2	1	1
Consumer services	5.9	0.9	2.4	0.6	0.6	0.2	7.3	0.8	—	—	4
Social services	15.8	0.6	14.5	0.7	16.6	0.6	13.2	0.7	—	—	4
Public administration	6.6	1.4	5.4	1.2	13.0	1.2	1.9	0.8	3	—	1
Other	0.2	1.0	0.3	1.9	1.5	1.9	2.7	1.7	3	1	—
Total	100.0		100.0		100.0		100.0				
E/P	0.67		0.66		0.69		0.76				
Suburbs											
Construction	9.1	1.5	8.9	1.7	11.9	1.7	8.4	1.7	4	—	—
Manufacturing	19.3	1.1	27.7	1.2	30.1	1.1	29.6	1.2	4	—	—
TCU	13.5	1.3	6.8	1.1	9.6	1.4	8.8	1.2	4	—	—
Wholesale	5.2	1.2	4.4	1.1	3.1	1.0	4.3	1.1	3	1	—
Retail	14.3	1.0	15.7	0.9	14.2	0.9	13.9	0.9	—	1	3
FIRE	7.4	0.8	8.2	0.8	4.3	0.6	5.3	0.8	—	—	4
Business/repair service	6.5	1.1	7.3	1.2	7.5	0.9	7.7	1.1	3	—	1
Consumer services	1.9	0.7	2.3	0.7	2.8	0.9	4.1	0.8	—	—	4
Social services	16.3	0.7	14.1	0.7	10.5	0.6	12.4	0.6	—	—	4
Public administration	5.8	1.3	2.9	1.2	4.7	1.3	4.0	0.9	3	—	1
Other	0.5	0.9	1.7	1.5	1.4	1.6	1.6	1.7	3	—	1
Total	100.0		100.0		100.0		100.0				
E/P	0.81		0.85		0.82		0.78				

Note: The concentration ratio is the ratio of the share of male or female employment accounted for by a given industry to the share of city or suburb total employment (both sexes) accounted for by that industry.

Source: Compiled from Current Population Survey data supplied by the Bureau of the Census.

Table 5.7 Percentage Distribution and Concentration Ratios (C/Rs) of Female Employed Residents by Industry, 1985

	New York		Chicago		Philadelphia		Los Angeles		Tally: C/Rs		
	Distribution	C/R	Distribution	C/R	Distribution	C/R	Distribution	C/R	>1.0	1.0	<1.0
City											
Construction	0.9	0.3	0.8	0.3	—	—	1.1	0.3	—	—	3
Manufacturing	16.2	1.1	14.8	0.7	14.3	0.9	16.2	0.7	1	—	3
TCU	6.0	0.6	9.2	0.9	3.7	0.5	5.3	1.0	—	1	3
Wholesale	2.1	0.7	3.5	0.9	2.5	0.9	3.3	1.0	—	1	3
Retail	9.3	0.8	17.7	1.0	12.4	0.9	14.6	0.9	—	1	3
FIRE	13.5	1.0	10.7	1.4	6.0	1.2	11.9	1.3	3	1	—
Business/repair services	8.3	1.0	8.3	1.1	7.7	0.9	6.1	0.7	1	1	2
Consumer services	6.9	1.1	5.0	1.4	4.5	1.8	11.7	1.3	4	—	—
Social services	34.3	1.4	26.3	1.3	40.6	1.5	26.9	1.4	4	—	—
Public administration	2.3	0.5	3.8	0.8	8.4	0.8	3.0	1.3	1	—	3
Other	0.2		—		—		—				
Total	100.0		100.0		100.0		100.0				
E/P	0.50		0.54		0.46		0.57				
Suburbs											
Construction	2.3	0.4	0.8	0.1	0.5	0.1	0.6	0.1	—	—	4
Manufacturing	14.1	0.8	17.0	0.7	19.3	0.7	18.9	0.8	—	—	4
TCU	6.9	0.6	5.6	0.9	3.3	0.5	4.9	0.7	—	—	4
Wholesale	3.5	0.8	3.3	0.8	2.9	1.0	3.7	0.9	—	1	3
Retail	14.4	1.0	19.9	1.1	18.1	1.2	17.0	1.1	3	1	—
FIRE	10.8	1.2	13.1	1.3	10.5	1.5	9.3	1.3	4	—	—
Business/repair services	5.7	0.9	5.1	0.8	10.0	1.2	6.2	0.9	1	—	3
Consumer services	3.8	1.4	5.2	1.5	3.5	1.1	6.0	1.2	4	—	—
Social services	34.6	1.4	27.9	1.4	29.8	1.6	27.7	1.5	4	—	—
Public administration	3.0	0.7	1.7	0.7	1.8	0.5	5.6	1.2	1	—	3
Other	0.7		0.3		0.2		0.1				
Total	100.0		100.0		100.0		100.0				
E/P	0.59		0.66		0.60		0.57				

Note: The concentration ratio is the ratio of the share of male or female employment accounted for by a given industry to the share of city or suburb total employment (both sexes) accounted for by that industry.

Source: Compiled from *Current Population Survey* data supplied by the Bureau of the Census.

Table 5.8 Percentage Distribution of White and Black Employed Residents by Industry, 1985

	New York		Chicago		Philadelphia		Los Angeles			Tally: C/Rs[b]		
	White	Black	White	Black	White	Black	White	Black	Other	W>B	B>W	W=B
Males												
Construction	6.0	4.7	7.2	0.8	8.5	1.6	5.7	5.1	2.2	4	—	
Manufacturing	13.4	9.8	28.3	24.6	16.6	19.7	26.2	20.0	21.8	3	1	
TCU	13.8	16.2	12.7	12.0	6.7	23.4	5.0	8.7	2.5	1	3	
Wholesale	4.1	2.5	5.1	3.7	1.9	5.5	3.4	3.6	2.5	2	2	
Retail	12.1	13.1	14.0	19.2	18.8	7.7	17.7	14.6	24.4	2	2	
FIRE	14.9	11.2	6.6	4.1	6.2	7.7	7.1	9.0	8.0	3	1	
Business/repair services	8.3	7.6	7.5	6.8	9.9	2.1	10.0	12.3	6.0	3	1	1
Consumer services	4.9	10.8	2.1	2.1	1.1	7.9	6.2	14.7	9.3	—	3	1
Social services	16.2	14.8	11.6	19.7	14.2	20.6	12.6	11.0	20.4	2	2	
Public administration	6.0	9.3	4.4	7.0	14.7	8.2	2.5	1.0	1.4	2	2	
Other	0.2	—	0.5	—	1.3	1.7	3.5	—	1.3			
Total	100.0	100.0	100.0	100.0	100.0	100.0	100.0	100.0	100.0			
E/P	0.71	0.55	0.76	0.55	0.77	0.67	0.82	0.66	0.66			
Females												
Construction	0.3	2.2	0.6	1.0	—	—	1.1	3.3	—	a	a	
Manufacturing	17.0	12.4	18.3	6.7	10.0	18.3	14.9	11.0	31.3	3	1	
TCU	5.3	7.3	6.6	13.5	3.0	4.8	5.1	5.2	6.3	—	3	1
Wholesale	2.2	1.2	3.9	1.8	2.2	2.9	3.5	1.7	3.4	3	1	
Retail	9.7	6.9	18.3	17.8	19.0	5.1	16.6	7.4	13.9	4	—	
FIRE	15.2	9.5	11.9	9.8	4.9	7.5	11.9	14.5	5.9	2	2	
Business/repair services	8.7	7.7	11.6	2.2	7.3	7.8	6.8	4.6	—	3	1	
Consumer services	6.4	8.4	5.1	7.2	3.8	7.4	13.3	5.1	8.3	2	2	
Social services	33.1	40.3	20.9	34.4	42.5	34.4	25.0	33.1	30.8	1	3	
Public administration	1.7	4.2	2.7	5.8	7.2	11.7	1.9	14.0	—	—	4	
Other	0.2	—	—	—	—	—	—	—	—			
Total	100.0	100.0	100.0	100.0	100.0	100.0	100.0	100.0	100.0			
E/P	0.51	0.48	0.58	0.48	0.56	0.38	0.62	0.48	0.47			

a Insufficient information for analysis.
b Actual concentration ratios are not shown in this table. See Table 5.7 for definition of concentration ratios.

Source: Compiled from Current Population Survey data supplied by the Bureau of the Census.

in three or more cities) in construction, manufacturing, FIRE, and business-repair services. Black men are relatively overrepresented (i.e., shares are larger than whites' in three or more cities) in two industry groups, TCU and consumer services. The first of these is made up largely of organizations in which affirmative action has been pursued fairly aggressively (the large utilities, communications firms, airlines, etc.). The second, consumer services (which includes personal services and hotels), is characterized, however, not by aggressive affirmative action but by the employment of large numbers of so-called service workers (most of relatively low skill). Moreover, it is an industry group with low average earnings. Thus, black male workers appear to have found easier access where either special employment policies favored them or where there was an above-average demand for unskilled labor.

Black women in the city tend to be underrepresented (i.e., shares are smaller than whites' in three or more cities) in manufacturing, wholesaling, business-repair services, and, in all comparisons, in retailing. They tend to be overrepresented (i.e., shares are larger than whites' in three or more cities), like black men, in TCU and in social services, where health services, in particular, offer large numbers of low-paying jobs. Black women also do relatively well compared to white women in public administration, with employment shares larger than white women's in all four cities.

Educational Attainment Characteristic
by Industry

Data on levels of educational attainment provide insight into the variations among industries in terms of the skill and experience levels of the persons they employ: Industries with a high percentage of college-trained workers presumably are more demanding in terms of skills and training of workers than those with a low percentage.

Tables 5.9 and 5.10 present separately for males and for females at each educational level a distribution of employment across industries. In each educational class, distributions of the four cities and suburbs are juxtaposed for easier comparison. Because data for each sex are subdivided into thirty-three cells (eleven industry groups at three educational levels), the shares (percentages) are subject to significant sampling error. Yet when the data for the four metropolitan areas are considered together, a number of fairly well-defined patterns become apparent.

In interpreting the data, we should pay attention not simply to the size of the percentage share of employment accounted for by a given industry within a given cell but also to whether the percentage in

Table 5.9 Percentage Distribution of Employed Male Residents by Industry and Educational Attainment, 1985

	< High School NY/CH/PH/LA	≥ High School < 2 Years College NY/CH/PH/LA	> 2 Years College NY/CH/PH/LA	Tally of CRs > 1		
				< High School	≥ High School < 2 Years College	> 2 Years College
Cities						
Construction	10/4/7/5	6/8/7/6	2/3/4/5	4	4	2
Manufacturing	18/44/23/35	12/24/20/25	10/18/10/20	4	3	—
TCU	9/12/25/3	22/13/8/8	10/10/11/5	2	4	1
Wholesale	4/3/5/3	3/8/3/3	5/2/2/4	1	2	2
Retail	21/26/12/23	17/17/23/23	5/6/7/11	3	4	—
FIRE	9/5/7/4	13/2/—/4	18/10/11/11	1	—	4
Business/repair services	10/4/8/9	7/8/11/11	7/10/6/10	2	3	2
Consumer services	7/1/4/5	5/2/1/9	6/4/—/7	2	1	1
Social services	9/2/10/3	8/12/9/7	28/27/32/24	—	—	4
Public administration	2/—/—/1	7/5/16/2	8/10/13/3	—	3	4
Suburbs						
Construction	14/11/12/12	12/13/15/11	5/4/5/4	4	4	—
Manufacturing	24/40/22/44	20/30/33/26	17/23/28/25	3	4	2
TCU	13/3/11/3	18/10/12/13	9/5/5/8	2	4	1
Wholesale	4/3/2/4	4/5/2/3	6/4/6/5	1	1	4
Retail	29/22/25/16	17/15/14/19	8/14/8/7	4	2	—
FIRE	1/4/1/0	5/4/3/4	11/13/9/11	—	—	4
Business/repair services	6/9/9/5	6/8/9/10	7/7/4/7	3	4	3
Consumer services	1/4/9/6	3/2/2/3	2/2/2/4	2	—	—
Social services	5/2/5/5	9/8/5/6	26/24/22/22	—	—	4
Public administration	—/—/—/2	5/4/3/3	8/3/9/7	—	4	4

Note: Underlines indicate CR > 1 (i.e., industry share of educational attainment group employment exceeds industry share of total employment.

Source: Compiled from Current Population Survey data supplied by the Bureau of the Census.

Table 5.10 Percentage Distribution of Employed Female Residents by Industry and Educational Attainment, 1985

	< High School NY/CH/PH/LA	≥ High School < 2 Years College NY/CH/PH/LA	> 2 Years College NY/CH/PH/LA	Tally of CRs > 1		
				< High School	≥ High School < 2 Years College	> 2 Years College
Cities						
Construction	1/2/—/—	1/1/—/3	1/—/—/1	—	—	—
Manufacturing	33/27/36/36	14/18/12/12	12/5/—/9	4	—	—
TCU	1/7/5/4	8/10/5/7	5/8/—/5	—	1	—
Wholesale	1/6/—/3	2/3/2/3	3/2/4/4	1	—	2
Retail	16/19/15/22	12/20/19/16	4/14/—/11	4	4	—
FIRE	5/7/4/2	20/12/6/15	9/12/6/13	—	3	2
Business/repair services	13/8/14/3	4/6/7/6	10/10/3/8	3	—	3
Consumer services	10/16/11/20	5/3/4/11	8/4/3/8	4	1	1
Social services	19/8/16/10	30/23/31/24	45/40/80/38	—	4	4
Public administration	1/0/—/—	2/4/14/4	3/5/3/4	—	1	2
Suburbs						
Construction	4/—/—/—	3/1/1/1	1/1/—/0	—	—	—
Manufacturing	30/27/20/32	16/17/22/21	9/12/12/11	3	2	—
TCU	6/4/—/1	9/8/5/7	5/3/2/4	—	3	—
Wholesale	—/3/1/2	4/4/3/5	4/2/3/3	—	4	—
Retail	18/32/42/20	18/23/17/23	8/13/11/9	4	4	4
FIRE	—/5/—/1	11/16/14/10	12/12/7/12	—	4	2
Business/repair services	2/3/4/5	3/6/11/6	9/5/9/6	—	1	1
Consumer services	15/11/18/16	5/5/3/4	1/3/3/5	4	2	4
Social services	20/14/11/18	26/18/22/18	47/46/51/42	—	2	4
Public administration	3/1/2/5	4/2/1/5	3/2/3/6	1	1	2

Note: Underlines indicate CR > 1 (i.e., industry share of educational attainment group employment exceeds industry share of total employment.

Source: Compiled from Current Population Survey data supplied by the Bureau of the Census.

question is larger than the comparable percentage for all workers, male and female combined, in the city or suburb represented. This is indicated by an underline in the tables.

Men. Inspection of the measures provides several findings pertaining to men:

1. In both city and suburbs, men with two or more years of college are relatively heavily employed (compared to those with lesser education) in FIRE, social services, and public administration, and, in the suburbs, in wholesaling and business-repair services as well. In social services and in FIRE, the differences are striking. Social services account for 24 to 32 percent of all employment of the top educational group in cities (22 to 26 percent in suburbs) compared to 2 to 12 percent of the city employment of the two lower attainment groups (2 to 9 percent in suburbs). FIRE accounts for 10 to 18 percent of the employment of the top educational group in cities (9 to 13 percent in suburbs) compared to 4 to 9 percent city employment of men with less than a high school education (0 to 4 percent in suburbs). Men with two or more years of college are also fairly heavily employed in manufacturing (10 to 20 percent or more of their employment in cities, 17 to 28 percent in suburbs), though to a lesser extent than in the lower attainment groups.
2. Men with less than a high school education are relatively heavily represented in most or all cities and suburbs in construction, manufacturing, and retailing, and, in suburbs, in business-repair services as well. On the other hand, they tend to find relatively little employment in wholesaling, public administration, and, as noted above, in social services and FIRE. The poor representation in FIRE is particularly unfavorable to employment of those with little education in the city, but the overrepresentation in construction, manufacturing, and retailing favors such workers in the suburbs.
3. Although the distributions of employment for men with high school training but less than two years of college are similar to those of men with less than a high school diploma, employment shares are somewhat smaller in manufacturing and retailing in most cities and suburbs and larger everywhere in public administration. We also observe that this middle educational attainment group is more heavily employed in TCU in both cities and suburbs.

In assessing the significance of these findings we must once again keep in mind that what is being examined is the distribution of the jobs of those who have found employment. We learn nothing about those who have not. But the distribution data do have implications for employability. That employed males with the least education are most restricted in terms of industries into which they find jobs implies that poorly educated men as a group find fewer opportunities for work than they would if they were more fully qualified to compete for jobs across the spectrum of industries.

Accordingly, it is important to note what has been happening in the cities in those industries most favorable and those least favorable to the employment of the poorly educated male. Among the least favorable, FIRE and social services have burgeoned in recent times, and government employment, though relatively static, has continued to be a major employer. Retailing, manufacturing, and construction—the most favorable—have not grown, at least in these cities. Thus, the developmental patterns of the cities appear to have been unfavorable for the employment of men with the least education.

The interpretation is quite different for men with the most education. As a group, they have found little difficulty in gaining employment (i.e., E/P ratios are high), and the relatively heavy concentration of jobs in certain industries simply tells us where the best jobs are to be found.

Women. When we interprete the industrial distribution of women's employment, it is important to keep in mind the earlier finding that E/P ratios are lower for women than for men in every educational attainment group (Table 5.4). These lower E/P ratios reflect not only differences in the demand for female labor but also differences in the willingness of women to seek employment in light of responsibilities in the home. Nevertheless, it is important to determine the extent to which women's employment is distributed differently among industries than men's and to observe the way in which educational achievement affects this distribution.

The most striking observations relating to women with two or more years of college is that employment is very heavily concentrated in social services, with shares of total employment ranging from 38 to 80 percent in cities and 42 to 51 percent in suburbs. Among the remaining industries, employment shares are for the most part low relative to comparable shares of employment for all workers. The principal exceptions are in FIRE, where the better-educated women are overrepresented in three cities and in all suburbs, and in business-repair services, where they are overrepresented in three cities and two suburbs.

The evidence here strongly supports the general contention that educated women find that opportunities for jobs commensurate with their training are more restricted than for men with the same educational qualifications. Nevertheless, women with college degrees do enter the work force in large numbers—their E/P ratios are high relative to those for women with less education. The finding thus relates to the extent to which they gain access across the range of industries, not to their ability simply to find employment.

Among women with less than a high school degree, as among men, employment is relatively concentrated in retailing, consumer services, and manufacturing, industries that are relatively more important in suburbs than cities. These poorly educated women are also overrepresented in business-repair services in three cities.

Employment of women with a high school education but less than two years of college is less concentrated in manufacturing and significantly more concentrated in FIRE and social services than is the case for those without a high school diploma. Of particular interest is the observation that in all comparisons the share of employment in FIRE is higher for workers with this level of education than for those with less schooling. These women, apparently, find their way much more readily into the secretarial pools or back-office factories of the banks and insurance companies than do those with less education.

The Significance of Part-Time Work

As useful as it is to indicate where men and women find jobs, the industrial distribution of employment in itself tells us nothing about the quality of employment—the extent to which men and women find well-paying, dependable jobs. Lacking information on wages, we must look to data relating to full- or part-time employment. Although part-time employment may be for some more desirable than full-time work—and this is most likely to be true for women who have responsibilities in the home—for many it represents simply lower pay and little or no opportunity for advancement.

Information regarding full-or part-time work is gathered from the CPS sample by asking each respondent classified as employed how many hours he or she worked in the preceding week (35 hours or more, 25–34 hours, 1–24 hours, not at work). In this analysis, all those working 35 hours or more have been classified as full time; those working less than 35 hours, as part time.

The principal finding is that the percentage of jobs worked on a part-time basis was larger for women than for men in every city and suburb (Table 5.11). A second finding is that in New York, Chicago, and Philadelphia a larger percentage of women worked part time in the suburbs than in the city, whereas for men there was little difference. In Los Angeles, however, part-time work was of roughly equal importance in women's jobs in city and suburb and somewhat more important for men's jobs in the city.

Table 5.11 Percentage of Male, Female, and Total Employed Residents Working Fewer Than 35 Hours by Industry, 1985

	New York			Chicago			Philadelphia			Los Angeles		
	Total	Males	Females	Total	Males	Females	Total	Males	Females	Total	Males	Females
City												
Construction	8.9	8.5	0.0	12.3	6.6	0.0	13.2	13.2	0.0	20.9	20.4	18.7
Manufacturing	8.1	7.2	8.9	11.5	10.6	13.4	2.2	0.0	5.4	9.3	8.0	12.0
TCU	4.9	3.4	9.2	14.7	19.0	8.3	3.9	4.9	0.0	13.0	15.6	9.3
Wholesale	1.1	0.0	3.5	6.9	0.0	16.8	0.0	0.0	0.0	19.8	19.8	19.9
Retail	26.9	18.1	40.8	32.6	21.9	42.5	30.8	28.7	33.6	32.9	22.8	49.4
FIRE	6.7	4.5	9.2	20.1	21.9	19.1	37.3	29.1	44.3	16.3	14.3	18.0
Business/repair services	19.6	14.7	24.8	21.0	9.8	32.0	31.1	21.2	44.7	17.4	12.7	28.2
Consumer services	28.0	17.0	38.8	41.3	0.0	59.0	38.5	56.3	33.4	24.1	16.0	31.2
Professional services	18.2	12.6	21.2	21.0	25.6	18.3	31.0	22.1	35.2	24.1	19.8	27.1
Public administration	6.5	5.2	10.6	3.4	0.0	8.9	10.7	0.0	27.5	9.2	8.7	9.7
All industries	14.2	9.4	19.6	19.3	14.6	24.3	21.3	14.2	29.2	19.7	15.2	25.8
Suburbs												
Construction	4.0	4.7	0.0	10.9	11.6	0.0	14.2	14.2	0.0	14.5	15.3	0.0
Manufacturing	11.3	8.1	17.1	11.5	7.8	19.5	7.2	3.6	14.8	7.5	4.6	13.2
TCU	16.1	8.1	35.7	10.9	4.7	20.5	12.5	12.4	13.0	8.8	4.2	19.7
Wholesale	12.1	8.2	19.3	12.5	3.6	28.4	3.3	5.4	0.0	5.8	2.0	11.3
Retail	42.2	27.7	61.4	44.6	28.2	60.9	47.5	34.2	61.9	31.8	23.5	40.6
FIRE	17.8	1.7	33.0	16.8	11.0	21.4	10.1	5.4	12.9	19.9	12.9	25.6
Business/repair services	15.3	6.8	29.2	26.2	18.6	40.9	28.3	15.4	41.8	15.3	12.6	19.7
Consumer services	28.5	8.6	44.4	44.9	36.6	49.7	57.3	62.0	53.3	37.3	32.4	41.5
Professional services	23.4	8.4	32.9	29.6	11.4	41.7	28.2	9.1	37.4	25.5	12.1	33.1
Public administration	10.5	2.7	29.4	3.3	0.0	11.1	11.0	0.0	34.2	6.2	2.5	9.4
All industries	20.2	9.9	34.1	23.4	12.9	37.0	23.2	14.5	35.0	17.8	11.0	26.6

Source: Compiled from Current Population Survey data supplied by the Bureau of the Census.

A third finding is that the lower levels of part-time work for men than for women were found in virtually every comparison at the industry level in both city and suburbs. For both men and women, the percentage of part-time work was *relatively* high in retailing in all cities and suburbs, although women's percentages were everywhere higher than men's. There were large variations among cities and among suburbs in a number of industries, however. For example, in New York City's FIRE sector, where employment is relatively large and average earnings quite high, part-time employment accounts for only 6.7 percent of all jobs, whereas in the other three cities it is significantly higher—particularly in Philadelphia, where part-time employment accounts for over 37 percent of all FIRE jobs.

Significance of the Analysis

Collectively, the preceding analyses provide evidence of critical problems facing poorly educated blacks—especially young black males—in the central city. In a recent article, John Kasarda has provided evidence based on the 1970 and 1980 Census of Population Public Use-Microdata Sample files to show how black employment opportunities have deteriorated in central cities in light of three major developments:[3] (1) the changing industrial structure of the city, in which jobs traditionally held by blacks—especially blue-collar jobs—have declined sharply; (2) the general decline in jobs available to poorly educated workers; and (3) the greater difficulty faced by blacks (especially young blacks) than by whites in gaining employment where jobs are opening up at some distance from their residence, i.e., in the suburbs. As regards the latter, his data show that lesser-educated young blacks are more dependent on private vehicles to reach suburban work than similarly qualified whites and that among young blacks those who resided in households without private vehicles were predominantly unemployed.

In another recently published article, Keith Ihlanfeldt and David Sjoquist have adduced impressive new evidence (based on studies of Philadelphia, Chicago, and Los Angeles) that among youths the probability of gaining employment is strongly related to distances of jobs from residence and that job access probability is significantly worse for black than for white youth.[4]

This research strongly supports a central thesis of this study. The recent developmental trends within large metropolitan economies have been of such a nature that central cities have narrowed the focus of their specialization, upgrading those sectors in which they enjoy greatest comparative advantage and thereby offering fewer employment opportunities for the poorly educated, especially disadvantaged blacks. The suburbs, on the other hand, have been growing rapidly, broadening the range of job opportunities. Although new strength is observed in the suburbs in certain of the business and social services, they nevertheless retain a strong orientation toward residentiary activities that provide employment opportunities for workers with poorer skill qualifications and inferior education.

At the same time, poorly educated and hard-to-employ minorities are located predominantly in the central city, where access to suitable employment is severely limited. In the next and final chapter we examine problems relating to housing and transportation that face both central city and suburb and examine certain significant differences between the employment experience of blacks and immigrant workers.

Notes

1. The reader should keep in mind that these E/P ratios are based on employment of residents in city or suburb (regardless of where employment took place) rather than employment at place of work, as in Table 4.2.

2. The concentration ratio is the ratio of the share of male or female employment accounted for by a given industry to the share of total employment accounted for by that industry.

3. John D. Kasarda, "Urban Industrial Transition and the Underclass," *Annals, AAP55* 501(January 1989):26–47.

4. Keith R. Ihlanfeldt and David L. Sjoquist, "Job Accessibility and Racial Differences in Youth Employment Rates," *American Economic Review* (March 1989):267–76.

6

Problems in City
and Suburban Labor Markets

This chapter summarizes the major labor market problems of central cities and suburbs and examines possible directions for public policy.

Problems Facing the Central City

In the competition between central cities and suburbs, the cities have traditionally enjoyed the advantage of cheek-by-jowl agglomeration economies, a more highly developed capital infrastructure, and superior access to a diverse labor market. But with continuous, relatively rapid growth of the entire postwar period, suburban economies have matured and broadened the range of industrial specialization. Moreover, the evidence of Chapter 4 indicates that the development of new business centers in the suburbs makes possible agglomeration economies not previously available and thereby strengthens the competitive position of the suburbs.

Under such conditions the central city faces new and stronger challenges from the suburbs. It must continuously hold on to its comparative advantages and revitalize its economy by attracting new firms. That a number of major cities have been able to successfully renew themselves is largely because the rapidly changing national economy is demanding new high-level services associated with new modes of finance, increased internationalization of trade, and new corporate organizational arrangements and needs.

In the recent past, the major thrust of developmental policy in the central city has been the rebuilding of the central business district. Much remains to be done along these lines, including the improvement of the physical environment and provision of more modern telecommunication infrastructures to facilitate the utilization of the new electronic technology.

But the critical need would appear to be the strengthening of the CBD's supply of skilled and adequately educated workers. Given the fact that such workers reside disproportionately in the suburbs, that suburban economies are expanding, and that commutation *within* the suburbs is increasingly popular, central city economies must suffer if they cannot draw more readily upon their own populations as well as upon the suburban labor force.

The overwhelming impression gained from a close examination of the economic and social indicators of the largest U.S. cities is one of a profound duality. On one hand, analysis of the employment and earnings data indicates that these cities have weathered difficult transformations and are moving toward greater specialization as service-oriented economies in which there is an upgrading of activities measured in terms of average earnings—some cities of course, more successfully than others. Moreover, within these cities there has been some movement toward gentrification (not withstanding the fact that in-commuting has continued to increase) and a marked upgrading of the residentiary sector in at least a part of the city, bringing about an increase in upscale housing, a refurbishing of retail stores and restaurants, and a new emphasis on cultural activities. On the other hand, there is a very large group of city residents living in poverty, homeless or inadequately housed, poorly educated, frequently unemployed, and often unemployable.

What we are observing are dual problems within the labor market stemming from the fact that a large part of the central city's potential work force is not equipped in terms of education and social skills to fill the kind of jobs that are available. The first is the problem facing employers. Failing to find acceptable workers within the city's labor force, they are frequently unable to fill job vacancies at economic wage levels by hiring suburban workers, given the longer distances of commutation to the city and the ready availability of alternative employment in the suburbs. With an increasing demand for better-qualified workers and a shift toward higher occupational levels associated with upgrading the city's economy, recruitment problems within the city's economy can only worsen.

The second is the larger social problem faced by the city's poor, mostly minorities, of gaining meaningful attachment to the labor force, a problem that is exacerbated by the changing industrial composition of the city's economy.

The two problems are clearly related: Improving the employability of the city's hard-to-employ would provide an increased labor supply for city employers. But there are other possible alternatives with quite different outcomes. Providing greater access to low-level jobs in the suburbs might improve the lot of the city's poor without easing the labor shortages facing city employers or, quite differently, moving businesses to the suburbs might reduce the extent of labor shortages in the city while providing no new jobs for minorities and weakening the city's overall economy.

Problems Facing the Suburbs

Problems facing the suburbs are for the most part of a different kind. Suburban employers face not a shortage of skilled, relatively well educated labor but of workers willing to accept low-wage, frequently part-time, jobs in the large residentiary sector, especially in retailing. During earlier years, this demand was filled by the youth of the baby-boom generation and by housewives newly coming into the labor force. With the aging of the baby boomers and increased employment opportunities for both young adults and housewives in the developing sectors, there is an increasingly serious labor shortage facing a large number of firms and institutions within the traditional residentiary sector.

Moreover, the suburbs are not without their problems of the hard-to-employ. In suburban cities, such as Mt. Vernon, New York, and Camden, New Jersey, there are urban ghettos not unlike those of New York City and Philadelphia. For example, Robert Cervero in his recent book, *Suburban Gridlock*, has noted that, "several suburbs collaring both Chicago and Los Angeles, in fact, have become predominantly minority communities over the past 15 years. . . . All 20 of the most economically distressed suburbs outside of Los Angeles, for example, are predominantly enclaves."[1] Within these communities, difficulties of gaining employment are exacerbated by problems arising out of the spatial organization of the suburban economy: Job openings are frequently located at points quite distant from the homes of the poor, and transportation is inadequate or excessively expensive.

The Housing-Job Mismatch

Indeed, the problems of spatial arrangement of housing and jobs are by no means confined to the poor in suburban ghettos. Heavy strains are being placed upon large numbers of the employed population by an inability to acquire conveniently located housing at acceptable prices and by a spatial organization of the suburban economy that places an increasingly heavy reliance upon commuting as a means of bringing workers to their daily jobs.

Housing has become progressively more expensive in the postwar years. In part, this has been because of the failure of improvements in construction technology to keep pace with improvements in other production technologies, in part because of the rising cost of land, and,

Table 6.1   Percentage Change in Population and Employment, Selected Suburban
Counties of New York, Chicago, and Philadelphia Metropolitan Areas, 1979–1987

	Population	*Employment*
New York		
Westchester	−0.3	+19.6
Nassau	+0.1	+22.6
Bergen	−2.5	+21.6
Chicago		
Du Page	+16.7	+55.2
Lake	+12.2	+25.8
Philadelphia		
Montgomery	+6.3	+24.0
Delaware	+1.7	+17.8
Camden	+4.9	+23.2

Source: Data supplied by the Bureau of Economic Analysis.

finally, because of increases in the standards of quality of housing acceptable in our modern society.[2]

According to à recent study, the price of land has contributed most to the rising price of homes. In 1949, land cost accounted for 11 percent of the cost of a typical single family home; by 1984, land cost had risen to 22 percent.[3] Frequently, the rising cost of land in the suburbs has been fueled by large lot zoning, by the unwillingness of communities to permit construction of multifamily housing, and by speculative withholding of land from the marketplace. In many of the inner suburban counties, population growth has been held virtually at a standstill, although employment growth has continued apace. Table 6.1 presents population and employment (farm and nonfarm) growth in the 1979–1987 period for the principal counties adjacent to the central city county in the metropolitan areas of New York, Chicago, and Philadelphia. Over this recent eight-year period, employment increased 18 to 55 percent in these suburban counties, whereas population change lagged far behind—6 percent or less in the New York and Philadelphia suburban counties, 12 and 17 percent in the two Chicago bordering counties.

Robert Cervero has pointed to five powerful economic and demographic forces that have contributed to the job-housing mismatch:[4]

1. *Fiscal zoning,* the practice of zoning land predominantly for high-revenue generating purposes, which has limited the supply of housing in certain areas and driven the price of housing upward.
2. *Growth restriction,* which includes placing a minimum-acre restriction on new housing permits, capping building permits, and placing a moratorium on growth.

Table 6.2   U.S. Commuting Growth Rates, All Modes, by Metropolitan Size Grouping, 1960–1980

Areas by Size (in millions)	All Central City	All Suburbs
>3	−4	84
1–3	47	151
0.5–1.0	20	122
0.25–0.5	40	106

Source: Alan E. Pisarski, *Commuting in America* (Westport, Conn.: Eno Foundation for Transportation, 1987). Reprinted by permission of the publisher.

3. *Worker earnings/housing cost mismatches.* The rising cost of housing (for all reasons suggested above) has pushed housing prices above the affordable limits of a large number of workers.

4. *Two-wage-earner families.* With husband and wives employed, it is frequently impossible to find housing located conveniently to the jobs of *both* earners.

5. *Job turnover.* Due to increases in career changes, corporate mergers, and plant closings, workers are finding it necessary to seek work at greater distances from their homes.

The result is that many people, especially young couples, are forced to find housing at locations far from the workplace. Herein lies the explanation of the rapid growth of population in the nonmetropolitan counties with heavy commutation into adjacent metropolitan areas, as noted in Chapter 1.

Commuting and Traffic Congestion

The rise in importance of commuting has been a principal characteristic of suburban economies, abetted by the increase in auto ownership and the construction and improvement of highways. During the two decades of 1960–1980, use of private vehicles as a mode of transport in the daily journey to work increased from 70 to 86 percent in the United States as a whole, and growth of suburban commuting (all modes) was far in excess of that in cities (Table 6.2).[5] In addition, the distance of the daily commute by suburban workers has lengthened (Table 6.3).

It is apparent that the predominant reliance on commuting to work by auto places a considerable burden upon the worker both in time and money. But it also places severe constraints on certain groups in finding acceptable employment. For example, wives in a one-car family may find the opportunity to hold a job ruled out unless suitable carpooling arrangements can be made or public transportation (typically limited in

Table 6.3   Average Trip Length of Suburban Commuters, 1980

	Average Trip Length, 1980 (miles)	Percentage Change in Trip Length, 1975–1980
Suburbs to		
Central city	12.2	+ 2.1
Suburbs	8.2	+17.1
Outside	19.2	+ 3.1

Source: Alan E. Pisarski, *Commuting in America* (Westport, Conn.: Eno Foundation for Transportation, 1987). Reprinted by permission of the publisher.

Table 6.4   Percentage Distribution of Average Peak-Hour Levels of Service for Main Arterial Highways and Main Freeways Serving 57 Suburban Centers, 1985–1987

Traffic Volume	Main Arterial	Main Freeway
A <60 percent (free flow)	3.5	5.5
B 60–69 percent (mainly free flow)	5.3	7.3
C 70–79 percent (stable flow)	28.1	20.1
D 80–89 percent (approaching unstable flow)	33.3	25.4
E 90–99 percent (unstable flow)	22.8	25.4
F 100 percent or > (jammed, forced flow)	7.1	16.4

Source: Compiled by Robert Cervero, based on survey responses and local engineering records. Robert Cervero, *America's Suburban Centers: The Land Use–Transportation Link* (Boston: Unwin Hyman, 1989), Figure 3.6, pp. 67, 71. Used by kind permission of Unwin Hyman Ltd. © Robert Cervero, 1989.

the suburbs) is available. In towns and cities in which there are substantial concentrations of minorities and the poor, the problems of gaining access to more than local jobs are likely to be daunting indeed.

But commuting difficulties are not simply the result of distance between home and workplace. As the volume of traffic has increased, congestion has rapidly developed as a major problem in the journey to work. In many suburban areas levels of traffic congestion have come to rival if not exceed any within or approaching the central city.

Developed by Cervero, measures of peak-hour levels of traffic for main arterial roads and freeways serving fifty-seven suburban centers provide some sense of just how congested many highways have become. Table 6.4 presents a percentage breakdown of average peak-hour levels of service on main roadways serving suburban centers. We observe that a third of main arterial roads operate, on average, at level D (80–89 percent of capacity), generally associated with congested conditions in suburban settings, and another 30 percent operate at even higher levels of congestion. For main freeways conditions appear to be somewhat worse, with over 40 percent operating at level E or worse.

Congestion impacts suburban labor markets both directly and indirectly—directly by adding to difficulties in the journey to work, increasing both time and monetary costs, and indirectly by increasing pressures upon local government to adopt zoning and other no-growth policies, which in turn accelerate sprawl, limit housing starts in areas close to employment centers, and raise housing prices.

Public Transportation

The problem of poor public transportation is closely related to the problem of excessive reliance on commuting. From the outset, the development of the suburbs was dependent on the family car and trucking. Housing, businesses, and institutions were often broadly dispersed.

Not surprisingly, the result has been poorly developed public transportation systems. On the one hand, the availability to most workers of a personal car as a means of getting to work reduces the general demand for alternative transport. On the other hand, the dispersion of both housing and workplaces further reduces the possibility of generating any considerable volume of traffic along any given route. The result has been that public transportation systems provide inadequate service—frequently offering no connection at all between home and workplace—and tend to operate at uneconomically low levels of traffic. According to a recent nationwide survey, only 2 percent of all suburban employees commute to work by bus.[6]

Lessons from the Immigrant Experience

Before considering possible measures to alleviate the labor market problems of central cities and suburbs it is useful to digress and to examine the experience of two groups of minorities in the central city: immigrants and blacks. There is evidence that the former have typically been more successful in gaining attachment to the labor force. Examination of the experience of the two groups provides insights useful in shaping policy to increase and improve the quality of minority employment.

Immigration into the United States has been unusually large in recent decades, with flows accelerating in the 1980s. During the 1965–1970 period, an average of 374,000 legal immigrants entered the country each year; between 1982 and 1986 annual inflows averaged 575,000.[7] For the most part, these newcomers have found a home in the largest metropolitan areas, with well over half of the immigrants who entered the country during the 1965–1980 period settling in the ten largest metropolitan areas.[8]

In a recent study based largely on interviews in the restaurant, garment, and construction industries, Thomas Bailey provides a number of insights into the experiences of immigrants in the New York City labor market.[9] Some highlights from among his findings follow.

1. The processes by which immigrants find work and attachment to the labor force are sharply different from those of native Americans, particularly blacks. They seek work where earlier immigrants of their nationality have found employment and with employers of their ethnic group. Though experience differs among ethnic groups, they tend to work as dishwashers, janitors and cleaners, low-skilled machine operators, or factory hands and newsstand clerks.

2. Living in ethnic enclaves and working within small paternalistic ethnic firms, they enjoy considerable job security as well as opportunities to learn more complex tasks and advance within the organization.

3. Though initially hampered by language problems and unfamiliarity with American culture and technology, they are not in a fundamental sense unskilled or untutored: Foreign-born individuals who arrived in the United States between 1975 and 1988 had on average almost twelve years of schooling.[10]

4. Immigrants have been relatively successful in becoming entrepreneurs in activities with low entry costs. Their success is in large measure due to their ability to make use of the same networking arrangements in recruiting workers that made possible their own earlier employment: They can draw upon the stream of new immigrants.

5. There is considerable evidence that immigrants do not compete with blacks in the labor market. The explanation lies in the fact that they find employment principally in secondary activities and in occupations in which blacks do not seek jobs.

In a more recent study, Thomas Bailey and Roger Waldinger examine the work experience of three groups (foreign-born Hispanics, foreign-born Asians, and native-born blacks) in New York City during the 1970–1986 period. They find sharp differences between the experience of blacks and the two immigrant groups and, to a lesser extent, between Hispanics and Asians.[11]

Although Hispanics were found to be heavily disadvantaged in the labor market in that they have been overrepresented in those sectors that were hardest hit in the declining economy during the 1970s—manufacturing, personal services, and retailing—their employment increased during the decade by over 50 percent. Today the composition of Hispanic employment remains roughly the same as it was in 1970, with virtually no movement into the expanding sectors of the economy. Among the reasons that Hispanics were able to expand employment in the 1970s was the massive exodus of whites that opened up more jobs in manufacturing for other ethnic groups than were lost by the sector's decline. In addition, "the small immigrant businesses that account for an important part of Hispanic immigrant manufacturing employment do provide some mobility opportunities for Hispanic immigrants; the continuation of this stream of immigrants provides the low cost labor supply on which those small businesses and the opportunities they represent depend."[12]

Foreign-born Asians were similarly overrepresented in retailing and manufacturing in New York City in 1970, yet the total number of these workers increased even more rapidly thereafter than did the number of Hispanic workers. Although their share of manufacturing remained constant, they became less dependent on retailing and were able to make gains elsewhere in the economy—in FIRE and in all of the white-collar occupations.

Like the Hispanics, the Asian immigrants were able to find employment by replacing the whites that had left the city. Moreover, they were strongly supported by the presence of well-entrenched ethnic businesses, particularly in the areas of garment production, restaurants, and food retailing. But their significant gains as professionals and in FIRE and business services reflects an increased integration of Asians into the broader economy, which the Hispanics for the most part did not share.

The black experience has differed sharply from that of Hispanic and Asian immigrants in New York City. The economic declines of the 1970s brought major job losses among blacks but at the same time significant transformation in the composition of their employment. Jobs were lost in personal services and retailing, but gains were made in FIRE, professional services, and government. The latter was of special importance: Over the decade there was a 23 percent increase in the proportion of native blacks employed by government. In summarizing the experience of blacks, Bailey and Waldinger note three major trends: "their growing concentration in public sector employment . . . ; their extensive transition from blue-collar to white-collar occupations; and the detachment of a growing proportion of male adults from economic activity."[13]

Bailey sheds considerable light on the black experience by examining the special characteristics of black employment and entrepreneurship.[14] He notes, first, that although blacks have found employment in the country's basic industries, which are characterized by well-organized internal labor markets, they do not have ready access to the informal networks available to immigrants in gaining access to employment in secondary job markets. Unlike immigrants, they must depend relatively heavily on formal labor market intermediaries to locate jobs.

Second, discrimination against blacks restricts their employment in those retail and service activities in which workers have contact with the public. For example, in the restaurant industry, Bailey found that employers tended to avoid hiring blacks as waiters, thereby weakening opportunities for these workers to move up to managerial or entrepreneurial positions.

Third, blacks have found easier access to employment in large organizations that, because of their visibility, have been targeted for strictest enforcement of affirmative action legislation.

Fourth, the lack of black-owned businesses is an obstacle for blacks in gaining attachment to the labor force. Here Bailey notes that the immigrant experience helps explain an important handicap of blacks in forming businesses: Black would-be entrepreneurs do not have access to a network that provides a stream of newly arrived immigrants who will work long hours at low wages. Moreover, he notes, "the lack of black owned sectors is self-perpetuating because potential entrepreneurs lack the opportunities for training and experience that immigrants enjoy in ethnic firms."[15]

Comparison of the immigrant and black experience serves to highlight a major problem facing many blacks: their difficulty in gaining meaningful attachment to the labor force. Unlike the newly arriving immigrant, the young black is not part of a social network that enables him to find work in a firm in which employment is relatively secure and in which there is visible evidence that over time there will be opportunity for advancement. Above all, he is unlikely to find a mentor in an owner-manager who has come up along the same route.

Clearly, the immigrant faces formidable difficulties of language, acculturation, and low income, but his hopes and expectations are sufficient to motivate him. In contrast, the young black from the ghetto may well find his early work experience meaningless. Admonitions to complete a high school education or to pursue even more schooling are likely to seem abstract and irrelevant in light of the casual employment with which he is familiar. The range of his observations provides little reason to expect that life holds more than one pointless job after another.

But there is another lesson to be learned. Regardless of the differences in black and immigrant experience, the fact remains that large numbers of both blacks and immigrants are congregated in our large central cities. Although it is important that all be able to move successfully into the world of work, it is not enough that they find employment in the secondary sectors or in casual jobs. There are many who have argued that the postindustrial city requires workers at all levels and that its vitality requires that all of these demands be filled. Surely this is true, but both the employment data and field research indicate clearly that for the central city economy as a whole there is an increased need for educated and more broadly adaptable workers who are qualified to become a part of the expanding primary sectors. The present situation in which workers must be increasingly drawn from the suburbs to fill middle-and upper-level jobs while ever larger numbers of the city's populace fail to even gain a foothold in the labor market or to move beyond the periphery of the economy is an invitation to weakness and decay.

Policy Alternatives

Essentially the principal routes along which policy might be implemented are twofold: (1) increasing opportunities for the poor of the central city to find jobs in the suburbs and (2) improving opportunities for hard-to-employ workers in both city and suburbs to more readily find employment without resort to long commutes or change in residence. The first type of approach includes opening up the suburbs through greater access to housing and improving opportunities for reverse commuting out of the city. The second includes improving job-market information, apprenticeships or on-the-job training, and strengthening the public education and training systems in both cities and suburbs.

Opening Up the Suburbs

The foremost advocate of opening up the suburbs to the city poor is Anthony Downs, whose major study published in 1973 best sets forth the importance and difficulties of using housing policy to create greater access among the poor to employment in the growing suburbs.[16]

Downs points out that in the United States acceptable ("decent") housing is defined by upper-middle-class living standards and is institutionalized in building and housing codes. He states that "nearly all new housing units in the United States (. . . excepting mobile homes) are too expensive for low- and moderate-income households to occupy— and even for many middle-income households"[17] and must be acquired as a result of a "trickle-down" process that he describes as follows:

When first created, the new neighborhood contains a cluster of housing units of basically similar quality, style, and price level. They were all built by a single developer or group of developers appealing to about the same market. The neighborhood is initially located near the edge of existing settlement in its metropolitan area. Also, it is initially occupied by households in the upper half of the national income distribution, because lower income households cannot afford to live there.

As time passes, the housing units in this neighborhood become older and less stylish compared to newer units. Housing fashions change swiftly in the United States—probably faster than anywhere else in the world. For example, the average size of new conventional single-family homes rose over 60 percent in eighteen years—from slightly under 1,000 square feet in 1950 to over 1,600 square feet in 1968. Design changes like family rooms, built-in appliances, and bathroom counter-top sinks also hasten the obsolescence of older units. Eventually their increasing age generates higher maintenance costs, too.

At the same time, the real incomes of many households initially living in this neighborhood increase. Many move to even newer housing units that are larger, more stylish, and in "fancier" neighborhoods. Gradually the edge of settlement moves farther out, leaving this neighborhood surrounded by other urban developments. This makes it relatively more central but also more hemmed in and subject to higher traffic congestion. In addition, relatively lower income households continuously move into the housing in the area. They are larger and tend to use the housing more intensively. For most incoming households, this housing represents an improvement over the even older units from which they have moved.

As more time passes, the once new housing becomes less and less desirable compared to the newest and best in society, even if it is well maintained. Because it is occupied by a succession of relatively lower ar.d lower income groups, it eventually houses groups with absolutely much lower incomes than those who first lived there. As long as the occupants have incomes high enough to maintain their properties, the neighborhood may remain in good physical condition. But in time, the annual costs of such maintenance become fairly high, while the occupants' annual incomes become quite low. Then the housing begins to deteriorate significantly. Households with alternative choices move elsewhere. Finally the housing becomes occupied by the lowest income groups in society and falls into extreme disrepair.

At that point, this housing has "trickled down" through society's income distribution from near the top to the bottom. Its life cycle results in its becoming a "slum" in three to six decades after it was built.[18]

An important characteristic of the process is that in new growth areas building or housing codes are rigorously enforced, in older neighborhoods they are less rigorously enforced, and in very low income areas they are almost totally unenforced—out of economic necessity resulting from the poverty of the residents.[19] Enforcement in the poorest areas would bring abandonment because residents are simply unable to pay rent that is high enough to provide returns to the landlord to pay taxes and provide a return on investment. Even without enforcement, abandonment has become commonplace in many of our older cities.

The trickle-down process then creates the ghetto and magnifies the burdens of the poor by concentrating them rather than allowing them to spread out through many neighborhoods.

What prevents the poor from moving into the suburbs is that suburban housing costs are high, mainly because there are legally required minimum standards for structure size, lot size, and building methods.[20] Moreover, these minimum size requirements and many construction maintenance requirements are based not upon health and safety considerations but upon cultural, political, and even personal economic considerations. Suburban residents are unwilling to see the poor admitted to their communities for a number of reasons, including a desire to retain a middle- or upper-income environment; an unwillingness to take on new tax burdens to provide for the additional educational and social services that would be involved by an in-migration of the poor; and a fear of falling property values, rising crime and vandalism, and a decline in the quality of schools.

Downs proposes a multipronged approach, involving opening up the suburbs and at the same time improving inner-city areas. Although a description of the details and an evaluation of his suggestions are not possible here, it should be stated that his proposals are predicated on a concept of voluntary movement of people and depend heavily on adequate subsidies for low- and moderate-income housing (including newly constructed units), macroecomomic policy to create a climate favorable to construction (e.g., low interest rates), and a marshalling of public opinion through strong political leadership.

Unfortunately, there has been little movement along the lines that were suggested by Downs more than one-and-a-half decades ago, although limited efforts have been made to break down zoning and other barriers to low-cost suburban housing. There has, of course, been a significant migration of middle- and upper-income blacks and other minorities into attractive suburban neighborhoods, but this has done nothing to relieve the problem of the inner-city ghetto. Indeed, in the eyes of many it has served to exacerbate the problem by removing from the scene successful members of the minority community who could have provided leadership and role models.

At this writing, there seems to be little likelihood of early action to open up the suburbs. Remedial measures to improve employment opportunities of inner-city minorities must involve other approaches.

Out-Commuting

As was shown in Chapter 1, there has long been a sizable commuter flow from central city to suburbs. These commuters, however, earn wages that are on average significantly above those of the city's poor. For the central city's disadvantaged workers, the obstacles to finding good jobs in the suburbs (jobs that pay better wages than, say, positions as domestic servants) are formidable. They include both lack of job-market information and costs and difficulties related to transportation.

City job seekers do not have ready access to information on suburban job openings. They are not tied in to the informal networking systems by which employers so often find job replacements and are unlikely to find openings through the city's public employment offices, which are poorly linked—if linked at all—to their counterparts in the suburbs.

Moreover, as noted above, public transportation in the suburbs is inadequate and often nonexistent. The heavy reliance on auto commutation effectively rules out many job opportunities for the poor city resident who does not own a car or cannot organize a car pool.

In recent years, there have been increased efforts to link poor city workers to the suburban job markets. In a few instances, housing projects have served as intermediaries between employers and job candidates and have organized van transportation that is available at cost. In other instances, large employers, such as McDonald's, have arranged for bussing of employees. Moreover, the increased importance of business centers of the sort described in Chapter 4 has increased the visibility of major employers and facilitated public transportation arrangements, as such centers provide destinations for a large number of riders.

Apprenticeships and On-the-Job Training

A major insight gained from the comparison of the experience of blacks and immigrants was that blacks face special problems in gaining attachment to the labor market within the central city because of a lack of social networks that lead to employment and of appropriate arrangements to maximize opportunities—once on the job—to gain experience, advancement, and expectations of success. This observation suggests that major efforts must be made *within* the central city or suburban job market through programs that involve employers and provide job candidates with better information as to where opportunities for work exist. Such efforts must incorporate arrangements for mediating the employment process along with incentives to employers to institute apprenticeships and on-the-job-training programs. An example of such a program that appears to have been quite successful is found at Murray Bergtraum High School in lower Manhattan. This high school, which specializes in business training, has established contacts with a number of firms in the nearby financial area who accept students well before the time of graduation. These students work after hours and during vacations under a carefully organized and supervised program and with the expectation of full-time employment and advancement after they receive their diplomas.

Education and Training

In the final analysis, any hope of moving large numbers of the unattached or marginally employed into positions as productive workers must rest on a more effective school system and the further development of training institutions such as vocational schools and community colleges to which workers can turn at any stage in their careers for remediation and acquisition of new skills. As this is written, there appears to be a new recognition that the educational system is performing inadequately and must be strengthened and broadened in a number of ways, including the recruitment of more effective teachers. Such a recognition is belated. The need is critical and must be met through more aggressive effort and substantially greater funding at all levels of the public sector.

Notes

1. Robert Cervero, *Suburban Gridlock* (New Brunswick, NJ: Center for Urban Policy Studies, 1988), p. 25.

2. The Ford Foundation, *Affordable Housing: The Years Ahead* (New York, NY: The Ford Foundation), pp. 13–19.

3. We shall see in a subsequent section ("Opening Up the Suburbs") that one analyst places greatest emphasis on the enforcement of high standards of housing quality as a major cause of high housing prices in the suburbs and a major obstacle to the filtering process that would otherwise make housing available to low-income workers outside the city.

4. Robert Cervero, *America's Suburban Centers: The Land Use–Transportation Link* (Boston: Unwin Hyman, 1989), pp. 49–51.

5. Alan E. Pisarski, *Commuting in America* (Washington, DC: Eno Foundation for Transportation, 1987), p. 44. Note that information on shares of modes of commuting is not given in the Pisarski study, but information on shares of families who do not own a car is provided. In 1980, 55 percent of zero-vehicle families lived in the cities; only 26 percent in suburbs. Pisarski, p. 34.

6. Cervero, *Suburban Gridlock.*

7. Roger Waldinger, "Immigration and Urban Change," *Annual Review of Sociology* 15(1989):211–232.

8. Waldinger, "Immigration and Urban Change," p. 215.

9. Thomas R. Bailey, *Immigrant and Native Workers: Contrasts and Competition* (Boulder, CO: Westview Press, 1987).

10. Bailey, *Immigrant and Native Workers*, p. 4.

11. Thomas Bailey and Roger Waldinger, "Economic Change and the Economic Division of Labor in New York City" (New York, NY: Conservation of Human Resources, Columbia University).

12. Bailey and Waldinger, "Economic Change and the Economic Division of Labor," pp. 26–27.

13. Bailey and Waldinger, "Economic Change and the Economic Division of Labor," p. 21.

14. Bailey, *Immigrant and Native Workers*, pp. 116–119.

15. Bailey, *Immigrant and Native Workers*, p. 119.

16. Anthony Downs, *Opening Up the Suburbs* (New Haven, CT: Yale University Press, 1973).

17. Downs, *Opening Up the Suburbs*, p. 3.

18. Downs, *Opening Up the Suburbs*, pp. 3–5. Downs notes that not all new neighborhoods undergo a life cycle. Some are maintained indefinitely, but the process is nevertheless widespread.

19. Downs, *Opening Up the Suburbs*, p. 6.

20. Downs, *Opening Up the Suburbs*, pp. 46–50. Downs, recognizing that there are old cities and towns in the suburbs where slums have been created, holds that this analysis is nevertheless largely applicable to central cities.

About the Book and Author

In this book fourteen large metropolitan economies are examined to show how industrial compostion and jobs have changed in central cities and suburbs since 1970. Driven by the shift in emphasis from goods toward services, both central cities and suburbs have undergone dramatic changes. The analysis shows that many large central cities have experienced wrenching transformations as a result of low growth or declines in employment and population. However, these cities have continued to be the focal point of economic activity within the metropolis, becoming more narrowly specialized in high-level services, which have yielded higher average earnings. These cities are becoming increasingly dependent on commuting suburbanites for their experienced and educated labor force.

In the suburbs, the cumulative effect of continuous growth since World War II has brought a different sort of transformation. The composition of employment has broadened, with sharp increases in commuting from areas outside the suburbs. Major new centers of business, consumer, and social services have developed, giving rise to agglomeration economies and posing new challenges to the social and economic structure of the central city.

The book also examines employment opportunities in central cities and in suburbs with special emphasis on jobs for blacks, women, and young workers. Analysis reveals the increasing importance of educational qualifications and the role of part-time work and focuses on the problems central city blacks face in gaining employment. The prospects for city dwellers seeking suburban jobs are often limited by housing and transportation restrictions. The book closes with a critical review of suggested policy alternatives that might increase access to employment for these workers.

Thomas M. Stanback, Jr., is senior research scholar, The Eisenhower Center for the Conservation of Human Resources, Columbia University, and professor emeritus of economics at New York University.

Index